Financial Crises

The financial crisis is a recurring phenomenon, yet its various instances have differed greatly in nature. Crises have punctuated the history of Western financial systems since the early eighteenth century, variously appearing in the guise of stock market crashes, large-scale failures of financial enterprises, collapses in the external value of a nation's currency or some combination of the three.

This study explores the major patterns of change in the evolution of financial crises as enduring phenomena, and analyses the paradoxical position that crises are at once similar to and different from each other. Brenda Spotton Visano examines economic, psychological and social elements intrinsic to the process of capitalist accumulation and innovation to explain the enduring similarities of crises across historical episodes. She also assesses the impact that changing financial and economic structures have on determining the specific nature of crises and the differential effect these have in focal point, manner and extent of transmission to other, otherwise unrelated, parts of the economy.

Financial Crises offers a consistent method for interpreting variations in financial crises through time and allows for a better overall appreciation for both the transitory fragility and enduring flexibility of financial capitalism and the potential vulnerability created by on-going financial development.

Brenda Spotton Visano is Associate Professor of Economics at York University, Canada.

Routledge Studies in the Modern World Economy

1 **Interest Rates and Budget Deficits**
A study of the advanced economies
Kanhaya L. Gupta and Bakhtiar Moazzami

2 **World trade after the Uruguay Round**
Prospects and policy options for the twenty-first century
Edited by Harald Sander and András Inotai

3 **The Flow Analysis of Labour Markets**
Edited by Ronald Schettkat

4 **Inflation and Unemployment**
Contributions to a new macroeconomic approach
Edited by Alvaro Cencini and Mauro Baranzini

5 **Macroeconomic Dimensions of Public Finance**
Essays in honour of Vito Tanzi
Edited by Mario I. Blejer and Teresa M. Ter-Minassian

6 **Fiscal Policy and Economic Reforms**
Essays in honour of Vito Tanzi
Edited by Mario I. Blejer and Teresa M. Ter-Minassian

7 **Competition Policy in the Global Economy**
Modalities for co-operation
Edited by Leonard Waverman, William S. Comanor and Akira Goto

8 **Working in the Macro Economy**
A study of the US labor market
Martin F.J. Prachowny

9 **How Does Privatization work?**
Edited by Anthony Bennett

10 **The Economics and Politics of International Trade**
Freedom and trade: Volume II
Edited by Gary Cook

11 **The Legal and Moral Aspects of International Trade**
Freedom and trade: Volume III
Edited by Asif Qureshi, Hillel Steiner and Geraint Parry

12 **Capital Markets and Corporate Governance in Japan, Germany and the United States**
Organizational response to market inefficiencies
Helmut M. Dietl

13 **Competition and Trade Policies**
Coherence or conflict
Edited by Einar Hope

14 **Rice**
The primary commodity
A.J.H. Latham

15 **Trade, Theory and Econometrics**
Essays in honour of John S. Chipman
Edited by James C. Moore, Raymond Riezman and James R. Melvin

16 **Who benefits from Privatisation?**
Edited by Moazzem Hossain and Justin Malbon

17 **Towards a Fair Global Labour Market**
Avoiding the new slave trade
Ozay Mehmet, Errol Mendes and Robert Sinding

18 **Models of Futures Markets**
Edited by Barry Goss

19 **Venture Capital Investment**
An agency analysis of UK practice
Gavin C. Reid

20 **Macroeconomic Forecasting**
A sociological appraisal
Robert Evans

21 **Multimedia and Regional Economic Restructuring**
Edited by Hans-Joachim Braczyk, Gerhard Fuchs and Hans-Georg Wolf

22 **The New Industrial Geography**
Regions, regulation and institutions
Edited by Trevor J. Barnes and Meric S. Gertler

23 **The Employment Impact of Innovation**
Evidence and policy
Edited by Marco Vivarelli and Mario Pianta

24 **International Health Care Reform**
A legal, economic and political analysis
Colleen Flood

25 **Competition Policy Analysis**
Edited by Einar Hope

26 **Culture and Enterprise**
The development, representation and morality of business
Don Lavoie and Emily Chamlee-Wright

27 **Global Financial Crises and Reforms**
Cases and caveats
B.N. Ghosh

28 **Geography of Production and Economic Integration**
Miroslav N. Jovanović

29 **Technology, Trade and Growth in OECD Countries**
Does specialisation matter?
Valentina Meliciani

30 **Post-Industrial Labour Markets**
Profiles of North America and Scandinavia
Edited by Thomas P. Boje and Bengt Furaker

31 **Capital Flows without Crisis**
Reconciling capital mobility and economic stability
Edited by Dipak Dasgupta, Marc Uzan and Dominic Wilson

32 **International Trade and National Welfare**
Murray C. Kemp

33 **Global Trading Systems at Crossroads**
A post-seattle perspective
Dilip K. Das

34 **The Economics and Management of Technological Diversification**
Edited by John Cantwell, Alfonso Gambardella and Ove Granstrand

35 **Before and Beyond EMU**
Historical lessons and future prospects
Edited by Patrick Crowley

36 **Fiscal Decentralization**
Ehtisham Ahmad and Vito Tanzi

37 **Regionalisation of Globalised Innovation**
Locations for advanced industrial development and disparities in participation
Edited by Ulrich Hilpert

38 **Gold and the Modern World Economy**
Edited by MoonJoong Tcha

39 **Global Economic Institutions**
Willem Molle

40 **Global Governance and Financial Crises**
Edited by Meghnad Desai and Yahia Said

41 **Linking Local and Global Economies**
The ties that bind
Edited by Carlo Pietrobelli and Arni Sverrisson

42 **Tax Systems and Tax Reforms in Europe**
Edited by Luigi Bernardi and Paola Profeta

43 **Trade Liberalization and APEC**
Edited by Jiro Okamoto

44 **Fiscal Deficits in the Pacific Region**
Edited by Akira Kohsaka

45 **Financial Globalization and the Emerging Market Economies**
Dilip K. Das

46 **International Labor Mobility**
Unemployment and increasing returns to scale
Bharati Basu

47 **Good Governance in the Era of Global Neoliberalism**
Conflict and depolitization in Latin America, Eastern Europe, Asia and Africa
Edited by Jolle Demmers, Alex E. Fernández Jilberto and Barbara Hogenboom

48 **The International Trade Sytem**
Alice Landau

49 **International Perspectives on Temporary Work and Workers**
Edited by John Burgess and Julia Connell

50 **Working Time and Workers' Preferences in Industrialized Countries**
Finding the balance
Edited by Jon C. Messenger

51 **Tax Systems and Tax Reforms in New EU Members**
Edited by Luigi Bernardi, Mark Chandler and Luca Gandullia

52 **Globalization and the Nation State**
The impact of the IMF and the World Bank
Edited by Gustav Ranis, James Vreeland and Stephen Kosak

53 **Macroeconomic Policies and Poverty Reduction**
Edited by Ashoka Mody and Catherine Pattillo

54 **Regional Monetary Policy**
Carlos J. Rodríguez-Fuentez

55 **Trade and Migration in the Modern World**
Carl Mosk

56 **Globalisation and the Labour Market**
Trade, technology and less-skilled workers in Europe and the United States
Edited by Robert Anderton, Paul Brenton and John Whalley

57 **Financial Crises**
Socio-economic causes and institutional context
Brenda Spotton Visano

58 **Globalization and Self Determination**
Is the nation-state under siege?
Edited by David R. Cameron, Gustav Ranis and Annalisa Zinn

59 **Developing Countries and the Doha Development Round of the WTO**
Edited by Pitou van Dijck and Gerrit Faber

60 **Immigrant Enterprise in Europe and the USA**
Prodromos Panayiotopoulos

Financial Crises

Socio-economic causes and institutional context

Brenda Spotton Visano

Routledge
Taylor & Francis Group
LONDON AND NEW YORK

First published 2006
by Routledge
2 Park Square, Milton Park, Abingdon, Oxon OX14 4RN

Simultaneously published in the USA and Canada
by Routledge
270 Madison Ave, New York, NY 10016

Routledge is an imprint of the Taylor & Francis Group

Typeset in Times New Roman by
Newgen Imaging Systems (P) Ltd, Chennai, India
Printed and bound in Great Britain by
TJI Digital, Padstow, Cornwall

British Library Cataloguing in Publication Data
A catalogue record for this book is available from the British Library

Library of Congress Cataloging in Publication Data
Spotton Visano, Brenda.
Financial crises : socio-economic causes and institutional context / Brenda Spotton Visano.
p. cm.
Includes bibliographical references and index.
1. Financial crises. 2. Finance. I. Title.

HB3722.S76 2006
332'.042–dc22 2005022974

ISBN10: 0–415–36287–3
ISBN13: 9–78–0–415–36287–0

Barb and Ron Spotton
Maria and Gino Visano

Contents

Preface

This book endeavours to explain financial crises. It strives to perceive the evolution of the crisis in its major contours as a first step towards a theory that allows explicit account to be taken of realistic ingredients. It is an evolutionary study in at least two senses. It examines the historical unfolding of events from initial innovation and speculation through to distress and panic. As well, it examines the changing nature of these events over time as that nature is influenced by (and influencing) the underlying financial structure in which instability occurs.

In theoretical finance, as in neoclassical economics, institutions and economic structure have receded far into the background. This study attempts to rescue the importance of institutions in defining the constraints that limit and pattern the behaviour of agents and to demonstrate how this behaviour of agents will, in turn, influence institutions. By examining the theoretical and historical dimensions of financial instability, this inquiry highlights the interplay between agency and institution.

Manias and crises share with institutions one very fundamental characteristic. Both owe their core existence to the presence of true or fundamental uncertainty of the type discussed by Frank Knight and others. Were all outcomes measurable and transaction costs negligible, we would observe neither institutions – as rules and conventions governing behaviour – nor the extreme market dislocations brought on by collective mania and panic. If for only this reason, it is fitting that the economic importance of institutions be explored in the context of an examination of extreme financial instability.

At a higher conceptual level, institutions exist in and because of a given structure. The dynamic between institutions and structure is an implicit dimension of this inquiry. In its simplest and crudest form, this study suggests that there exist thresholds that when crossed proximately cause a crisis. The crisis, in turn, initiates a process that can fundamentally alter the structure in which agents operate. The behaviour of the actors becomes increasingly aggressive over time; self-interested action is increasingly to the inadvertent detriment of the group. Further, the constraints that define the thresholds are themselves subject to agency influence in a manner that increases the risk of crisis as time passes. Institutional thresholds are, in other words, on a collision course with agents' behaviour; how these thresholds change over time is, then, critical to understanding the intrinsic dynamics of finance capitalism.

Ultimately, I am guided by the desire to further develop an understanding of financial instability that lends itself directly to policy statements and social commentary. One of the longest-standing objectives of financial regulation has been to minimise instability. Much of the regulation with which we are familiar was originally designed to create the main safeguards against the spread of a crisis. Financial systems are, however, changing dramatically because of political and corporate restructuring and technological advance. Pressure to remove or at least relax legislation has been and continues to be successful in the dismantling much of the regulatory structure that has been in place for decades. The arguments are, loosely, that the laws are outdated, now distorting market price signals and hindering financial progress. Consequently, full historical appreciation of the current relevance of existing regulation is critical, as is the fullest understanding of the theoretical underpinnings that inform these decisions. It is hoped that this study will contribute to a deeper and more fertile understanding of the phenomenon in a way that moves us closer to this goal. The work presented here is in many important ways preliminary. Consequently, the hypotheses contained in this book are best considered to be ones that are fluid, tentative and inviting further research.

The approach taken in this book is the product of a struggle with the discipline in which I was trained as much as a struggle with the topic itself. It is fair to say that the majority of economists labour under the belief that only the most recent of research represents the most advanced state of knowledge. This is of dubious validity in the context of economics. Rarely are students invited by their teachers to study the merits of earlier works steeped in neither mathematical equations nor statistical analysis. The word 'data' is, to the majority of economists, now synonymous with quantities, 'empirical' means to run regressions on data, and the 'formal' model is a mathematical one. Contemporary theoretical debates are now motivated more by the nuances of the mathematically arcane and statistically idiosyncratic and less by serious policy questions.

Put differently, economics, as a discipline, is at risk of realising the dangers of 'over-specialisation'. The culture is such that, increasingly, it empowers only those willing to adopt fashionable approaches, relegating alternative voices to the fringe or worse. The cost to all of us lies in the detrimental circumscription of the arena of debate and the severe constraint placed on the potential gains from exchanging ideas. History, history of economic thought, social and political thought, and the like have all been excised from economics programmes and graduate research; replaced by mathematical and statistical techniques applied to only those very narrow questions amenable to constrained optimisation, linear regression, game theory and the like.

Mathematical techniques and economic statistics now fill the economist's toolbox all but exclusively. While necessary and useful instruments for some purposes, like all specialised instruments, they offer greatest advantage when employed in concert with a multiplicity of complementary tools. Arguably, we have lost sight of the importance of, what Joseph Schumpeter called in his *History of Economic Analysis*, the other two 'fundamental fields' of scientific economic analysis – economic history (which Schumpeter considered *primus inter pares* and by which he meant analysis of a 'unique process in historic time', reflecting '"institutional" facts that are not purely economic') and economic sociology (where analysis extends to include social institutions that are relevant to economic behaviour such as government, contracts and the like). To the extent that specialised tools developed to support each of these four fields are, in some manner, or, at some times, working in opposition, we might observe the 'criss-cross' progress of which Schumpeter speaks.

In default of any well-specified, realistic dynamic process in historical time, mainstream economists have, overall, steadfastly adhered to models of (instantly) equilibrating, a-historical systems in atomistic markets comprised of homogeneous agents trading in isolation on costless, equally-valued information. That they have little to say about events that are inherently institutional and that are fundamentally the result of disequilibrium trades by heterogeneous investors with different and differentially-processed information is hardly surprising. Yet when actual financial conditions dictate special situations – such as those that define manias and crises – and vice versa, and when the level of financial activity determines and is determined by the underlying institutions and structures, we must, I contend, choose our abstractions in a manner more sensitive to that specificity.

The approach adopted here falls generally within the institutionalist approach in the sense discussed by Geoffrey Hodgson (1998) and Warren Samuels (1995), for example. Use is made of historical and comparative material concerning socio-economic institutions and processes for deriving stylised facts and theoretical conjectures concerning causal mechanisms. The complexity and historical specificity of the approach provide, quite clearly, major deficiencies as testable representations. Critical testing of simple causal linkages is impossible. Disequilibrium, path-dependency, structural shocks and qualitative changes of the type analysed here preclude any ability to confirm or refute many of the specific hypotheses. Moreover, as with all historically grounded explanations, the evidence is relatively sparse and ambiguous to be compatible with several, potentially contradictory, explanations of the mania–crisis phenomenon. The benefits of such an approach lie, nevertheless, in the fact that the resulting explanation of financial crises permits a clearer identification of transparent roles for credit, technology and institutions in evolving capitalist economies, thus making the awkward translation from theoretical model to social commentary easier. Or so I believe.

Acknowledgements

Any researcher, as a student past and present, owes both intellectual and moral debts to all those who have generously shared their ideas and insights, guidance and advice. Of the many from whom I have learned much beyond that which the written word has to offer, I owe the most special of debts to Tom Asimakopulos, Samuel Hollander and Robin Rowley. The late Tom Asimakopulos will always be most fondly remembered for his commitment to students, a commitment that matched his substantial commitment to Keynes' ideas and post-Keynesian research. Sam's enthusiasm for the history of ideas is infectious and his openness to revisiting the most basic of questions has been as refreshing as it has been encouraging. Robin's breadth of knowledge, his humour, and his iconoclasm make him an exceptional researcher and colleague. From him, more than anyone, I have gained, in particular, a better understanding of dynamic processes. They each have set a standard of scholarship that I greatly admire and can only hope to emulate.

Of the many colleagues with whom I have been fortunate to collaborate, in some fashion, or, to engage discussions on topics related to this study, I have specially to thank Luigi Bianchi, Bob Dimand, Omar Hamouda, Tom Kompas, Phil O'Hara, Chris Paraskevopoulos, Gideon Rosenbluth, Leslie Sanders and George Sciadas. I thank, as well, Yoko Furukawa, Marc-André Pigeon and Mark Setterfield.

My understanding of institutional change as an evolutionary process has benefited as much from my work for the university as it has from my focused research. As a senior academic administrator and, later, chief negotiator for one of the largest faculty unions in Canada, I experienced, first hand, the vital importance of social and political influences in defining and constraining such change. Of the many with whom I have had the pleasure and honour to work in these and other administrative capacities, it is Brenda Hart who deserves special mention. From our many hours of working together and thinking through the nuances, strategies and politics of labour relations, I have learned at least as much about the interplay between the social, the psychological, and the economic, as I ever did throughout the many years of my formal education.

To the students at York University in my undergraduate course in money and banking and my graduate course in financial crises, I extend my sincerest appreciation for their patient probing of ideas. All of these students were teachers, each in their own way, willing to challenge the status quo and to explore new territory. Students who deserve particular mention are Mohamed Abdelhady, Horatio Morgan, Chuck Niu, Alex Nikolic, Antonia Swann, Aqeela Tabassum and Xiaomei Zhang.

Barb, Ron, Maria, Gino, Beverley, Herb, Toby, Jim, Theresa, Nancy, Jeff, Franca, Tony, Rose, John, Fulvia, Wolf, Eloisa, Tammi, my many nieces and nephews and the memory of my brothers Doug and Franco are a constant reminder that life outside of the world of heterodox finance is full, rich and very precious. I extend a special thanks to Anthony. He is much more than a young man wonderfully curious, full of life, and often great as a check on reality; he is part of the next generation of financial speculators. In a way, this book is for him (which is not to say he will read it!). His enthusiasm for everything financial is exciting. But striving for any gain involves risk and, more important, forces us to confront uncertainty. The ultimate goal of this study is to render a bit more comprehensible that uncertainty and to understand a bit better that 'downside risk' – in the hope that future speculators might be a little more wary and a lot more aware of the broader implications of their actions.

I gratefully acknowledge the financial and in-kind support of York University, the York University Faculty Association, the Atkinson Faculty of Liberal and Professional Studies and the Faculty of Graduate Studies. I thank Beth McAuley for expert assistance in the preparation of this manuscript. Her suggestions for how to improve the communication of the book's message, as well as her attention to the details of writing, have greatly improved the readability of this text. For their administrative and moral support of my research and teaching, I thank Margo Barreto, Vanessa Broughton, Agnes Fraser, Ellis Lau and Elsie Ramkhelewan. Special thanks are due to Lara Ubaldi. Working with each of them has made, and continues to make, the privilege of a career as a university professor that much more enjoyable and rewarding.

Last, because he is first, I have most to thank Livio Visano. I am incredibly fortunate that my husband is also my closest friend, an exceptional scholar and an unconditionally supportive critic. As has every new endeavour I undertake, each chapter in this book has benefited immeasurably from our discussions. His collaboration on this project, though, extends well beyond anything I can itemise; rather, it is in the shape of the work itself and the very fact that exists in public form.

Part I

The socio-economic context

1 An introduction to the evolution of financial fragility

Financial crises of foremost concern are those financial disruptions that adversely affect the general well functioning (or an important part) of the economy. Financial crises may first appear as the dramatic collapse in the prices of marketable financial instruments or the insolvency of lending establishments and suspension of their credit facilities. The breakdown in financial markets or sudden withdrawal of credit can adversely affect on a large scale the day-to-day commercial operations of organisations in the non-financial sectors of the economy. In this way, financial crises can precede both temporally and causally economic crises in employment, production and trade. At the economic level financial crises are systemic disturbances to the financial system that impede the system's ability to allocate financial capital and disrupt the economy's capacity to function. Triggering a loss of economic value, the crisis impairs the economy's ability to allocate its resources, causing severe financial and economic distress. Triggering a loss in confidence, the crisis ushers in a state of normlessness, or Durkheimian anomie. Shattered is the feeling of certainty in action, and an anxious uncertainty replaces a prior confidence in comprehension.

Yet rarely are two historical episodes of crises identical. As some have argued, there is no single type of crisis.[1] Comparative analyses of historical crises typically offer taxonomies of the crises with types differentiated variously by sectors (public versus private or corporate arenas), objects of speculation or institutional spheres of finance (banks versus financial markets).[2] Comparative historical analysis has ventured little beyond the taxonomy to examine the manner in which the underlying institutional and economic structures may explain the variations. And there remains debate surrounding the relative importance of financial development versus financial structure in influencing the overall stability of the financial system (see Dolar and Meh, 2002). The challenge that remains is to explore a means of understanding the similarities common to all crises in a framework that is flexible enough to permit a consistent explanation of historical differences.

This study attempts to perceive in its major contours the evolution of the financial crisis as an enduring phenomenon that unfolds in historical time and that will transform itself in specific detail through time. The extent to which a crisis is the inescapable consequence of the economic and social elements intrinsic to the process of capitalist accumulation and innovation explains the enduring similarities of the crisis across historical episodes. The influence of the mutating financial and economic structures in which the crisis occurs ensures that the historical detail of each crisis will differ markedly in focal point, manner and extent of transmission to other, otherwise unrelated, parts of the economy. The key to understanding the seemingly paradoxical position that crises are at once similar to and different from each other lies in the role institutions play in the operation of the finance capitalist system.[3] By exploring the essential role of financial institutions in informing and transforming the financial crisis, this study attempts to achieve a consistent means of interpreting variations in financial crises through time.

Institutions are variously conceived of as a legal enterprise (such as a bank), a social practice (such as market exchange) or a system of rules as forms of constraint 'that human beings devise to shape human interaction' (North, 1990: 4).[4] While institutions may be informal as defined by custom or formal as defined by law, in this work I am concerned with those formal institutions that define the financial structure in capitalist systems and which, in the broader sense, operate to structure incentives and guide behaviour.

That financial crises are, in their essence, an institutional phenomenon demanding explicit location in the economic and financial structures in which they occur is not a new idea. Neither is it novel to suggest that an analysis of institutions can explain the differential performance of economies through time. Insofar as the present study grounds the existence of institutions on the human desire to create predictability in the face of uncertainty, permits the social construction of knowledge and understanding to define an outcome, examines financial crises as a fundamentally institutional phenomenon and explores the influence of institutions on the differential performance of the financial economy, the schema it proposes shares many features of extant institutional analyses of crises specifically and the relationship between structure of financial institutions and the economy more generally. Yet, to date, there is no study that seeks to combine the evolution of financial institutions, as a social construct, with the variations in the types of financial crises we can observe when looking back through history.

Whereas economic analyses of institutions and institutional change limit their focus to the rational individual who is constrained in ability to access and process information, the present study permits the intrusion of the social. In permitting the social to shape individual understandings and to inform individual actions in a manner consistent with the social interaction literature, the path along which both the crisis and the speculation that precedes it develop, becomes dependent on both the historical past *and* the collective understanding of the present.

Whereas studies that examine the relationship between the economy and its structure of financial institutions focus on explaining variations in longer-term rates of economic growth and development, this study applies the structural–functional analysis of the finance–economy relationship to the question of transitory crises. In this way, the present study retains the insights offered by extant institutional analyses of crises in a framework that permits the interaction between institutions and crises to evolve over time. The flexibility of the structural–functional approach permits, in turn, an analysis of crises in both the markets for financial instruments and lending institutions and, if successful, begins to bridge a gap that currently exists in the economic literature of crises.

In short, by combining research on social interaction in a capitalist system with a psychological–economic analysis of institutions and examining the relationship between financial institutions and financial crises in an evolving economy, this study brings together well-researched parts into a different whole. The hope is that by understanding better the interaction between the crisis and the underlying institutional structure in a social context, we might gain a better overall appreciation for both the transitory fragility and enduring flexibility of finance capitalism.

This study proceeds as follows. Following a brief tour of six historical crises occurring at various times in three different countries, the opening chapters of Part I explore the foundations of an institutional perspective on financial crises. Chapter 3 explores capitalism as a culture that values material wealth and focuses on material gain, innovation and accumulation. Chapter 4 explores the general nature of uncertainty and information. It examines the process of understanding the behaviour and examines the information and guidance available to decide what action to take when uncertainty about objective future outcomes prevents a calculus of probabilities from informing any cost–benefit analysis of material gain. Chapter 5 considers the rather unsatisfactory nature of traditional explanations of financial instability when orthodox explanations are confronted with their assumption of knowable future outcomes.

With the foundations of culture, innovation and behaviour established, and the deficiencies of traditional explanation exposed, the next three chapters of Part II explain the three primary dimensions of instability that appear common to all historical crises.[5] Chapter 6 explores the manner in which speculation via financial instruments financed by credit expansion at once facilitates the process of adopting the innovation and creates the fragility that foretells a crisis, Chapter 7 examines the role of credit in financing a speculation and the particular role of banks and Chapter 8 investigates the nature of the distress and the conditions under which distress degenerates into panic. In a world where future outcomes are neither known nor knowable, current and future prospects are contingent on collective understandings. This environment opens the door to an evolution in speculative investment and credit creation that is defined not by objective circumstances, as efficient markets theorists and pure monetarists would have it, but by subjective, path dependent developments that serves to increase fragility as the episode unfolds.

The last two chapters provide a sketch of a framework flexible enough to expose the differences in crises arising from institutional variations. Chapter 9 relates the nature of the financial crises to both the contemporaneous financial structure and the nature of the economic transition spawned by the contemporaneous innovations. Chapter 10 explores the use of balance sheet indicators of the financial structure and the networks of linkages represented in this framework and considers the extent to which the indicators may be reasonable and practicable for portraying and analysing historical crises. A concluding chapter offers some reflections and projections.

2 Illustrations of manias, panics and crises

History does not repeat itself... but it rhymes.
(commonly attributed to Mark Twain)

Episodes of financial crises punctuate the history of finance capitalism. Since the early beginnings of formal financial systems in the late 1600s, developing nations have periodically experienced episodes of fantastic speculative optimism followed by recoil in pessimism and calamity. Of the many episodes occurring intermittently throughout the last three centuries, six are briefly described later. These are simply six important episodes chosen as illustrations of a single phenomenon that varies in considerable detail over time and in an ever-widening global space.

Early eighteenth-century England

In the second decade of the 1700s, the English parliament sanctioned a radically innovative plan to privatise the government's burdensome debt. With the March 1720 passage of the Refunding Act, Parliament granted the South Sea Company permission to acquire government debt and to finance the acquisition by expanding its issue of company shares.[1] Easy credit terms (with subscriptions available for only a fraction of the market value required on purchase),[2] together with the uncertain promise of a great experiment never before tried, encouraged the initial speculation by leading members of Parliament, themselves encouraged by inducements paid by the South Sea Company to these persons of influence. Speedy and substantial price increases fuelled further excitement. A 'bubble' in the prices of the shares of the company holding the monopoly on the conversion ensued. A spectacular rise in the share prices of the South Sea Company rose to a peak of 1,050 pounds per share in August of 1720,[3] from a mere 128 pounds per 100 pound par value share the previous January.[4] By the end of

September, however, share prices had collapsed to around 200 pounds reaching a low point of 124 pounds in late December.

The speculation subsided with the enactment of legislation prohibiting the operation of unauthorised joint-stock companies.[5] It is common to point to the Bubble Act as the beginning of the demise of the South Sea Bubble and by the price estimates available, it appears that the rate at which prices increased in the remaining time slowed considerably. Initial reactions to the passage of the Act started a rush to liquidity, according to Davies (1994), which reached the state of a general panic by August. Ashton (1959: 119) identifies the issue of writs against unauthorized companies on 18 August, 'that brought the frail structure to the ground'.

With the slowdown and eventual decline in share prices, the debt burden of margined shareholders increased significantly. Although the collapse did not wipe out the Company itself, its directors and others involved in what was then viewed as general corruption were heavily fined, imprisoned and had their estates confiscated to help to compensate the victims of the crash. The principal creditor of the Company and major competitor of the Bank of England in the sphere of commercial banking, the Sword Blade Bank, failed in September of 1720. The failure of its primary competitor in commercial banking, and the diminished capacity of its primary competitor in government banking, secured the Bank of England's central importance in the London financial market.

While the 1720 financial crisis was remarkable and accounts of it are remarkably vivid, evidence suggests that the adverse impact, measured in terms of reported bankruptcies in otherwise unrelated activities, was minimal and remained limited to those directly participating in the sphere of public finance. Hoppit (1986), through careful analysis of bankruptcy totals, shows that bankruptcies 'moved above their trend line only once, in the final quarter of 1720', affecting the edifice of public credit all but exclusively. As these data would not reflect the distress of farmers and landowners, who by law could not be dealt with via bankruptcy, Hoppit implies that increased land sales marked the distress experienced by the naïve speculator and turns to E.P. Thompson's (1985 [1977]) account in *Whigs and Hunters*. 'It was the small speculator, the petty country gentleman or substantial farmer, jealous of the gains of his wealthy neighbours, who came late into the game, without experience and without London advisers, who was most likely to lose his all' (as quoted in Hoppit 1986: 48).[6]

Early nineteenth-century England

A century later, the rising democracies of the newly liberated South American countries in need of funds found ready suppliers in Britain.

The Latin American needs appealed to the new British political idealism and supporting commercial strategy that had developed during the profound transformation that marked readjustment to peacetime production following the Napoleonic wars. The South American opportunities for mining investment offered the principal speculative focus in 1822–1824.[7] Technological innovations that advanced the steam engine together with the profound social and economic transformation that advances in rail transportation stimulated, offered unparalleled investment opportunities in the subsequent two decades. Principal increases in stock-exchange dealings came from financing foreign loans and new infrastructure development (Morgan and Thomas, 1962). The declining rate of return on state debt created 'the feverish feeling in the minds of the public at large, which prompted almost everybody to entertain any proposition for investment, however absurd' (J.H. Palmer, then Governor of the Bank of England, as quoted in Gilbart, 1968 [1882]: 66).

The 1824–1825 stellar increase in the index of mining share prices reflects the public's enthusiasm for this investment opportunity. In October of 1824, the index first reports a value of 525. From most accounts (Tooke, 1838; MacLeod, 1886; Hyndman, 1967 [1908]), it was the promise of quick gain, based on initial success and enhanced by a nominal 5 per cent margin requirement, that started a mania at the end of 1824. Many, Jenks (1927) claims, were ignorant of the lack of any real potential. By January of 1825, the value increased by more than 500 per cent to 3326. The index declined slightly in the following two months before falling sharply in April and May. Between July and December of 1825, the period of peak commercial distress, the index lost more than half its value. By September of 1826, the index returned to it pre-boom level, however mining projects, one after another, had been abandoned in the interim.

The beginning of the end of the South American mining mania arrived when shareholders were approached for additional capital instead of being sent dividends; at that point, demand for shares slowed and prices stabilised. Speculators, unable to realise a profit before the next instalment came due, sold off assets and drove down share prices (Tooke, 1838). A contraction of country-bank credit was sparked, reportedly on the news that a Bristol bank had refused to convert its bank notes into gold on demand. The pressure on liquidity was exerted on the banks from the heavy loads of unusually long-dated bills and other securities (Clapham, 1945), and in mid-September of 1825, London bankers ceased lending on South American securities (Pressnel, 1956).[8]

The financial distress of this period is marked by the pronounced increase in bank failures across England. In the years spanning 1816 to 1824, banks failed at an average annual rate of 2 per cent but jumped to more than 10 per cent in the distress period Clapham (1945: 90). Initial failures appeared in 'demonstrably weak and insignificant' agricultural banks (Pressnel, 1956). The failure of a major London agency bank in December of 1825 began a run in 43 correspondent country banks, which spread to other banks in the same towns and finally to banks in nearby towns (Pressnel, 1956). By the end of 1825, 73 principal banks, 37 issuing banks and 60 country banks had failed, or nearly one-quarter of the number existing but one year previous. In addition, nearly half (12) of the 25 bill brokers failed in this time.

Middle nineteenth-century England

The railroad boom of the 1840s was associated with the amalgamation and consolidation of the main trunk system and shared a similar history with the earlier mining mania. Cheap money (with the Bank of England's discount rate consistently below a low market rate) and the promise of higher returns in railroad speculation 'developed in 1845 into an orgy of speculative activity that surpassed the excesses of 1824–5' (Ward-Perkins, 1950: 76; see also Boot, 1984).[9]

> Forty-eight Acts were passed by the House of Commons in 1844, 120 in 1845, 272 in 1846 and 190 in 1847, the last involving £40 million of new capital issues. In 1848 the capital sum dropped to £4 million... Panic occurred in 1847 when further capital calls, amounting to £16, 150,000 issued in a single month of January, found many buyers unable to pay and forced to dump shares. Initial down payments had seldom been higher than 10 percent.
>
> (Kindleberger, 1984: 200)

Prices of railway shares, however, peaked and crashed most noticeably two years earlier in 1845, with a 40 per cent rise and fall in share values over 11 months. From December of 1845 onwards, there was a steady downward trend that lasted through to the end of 1848 (Ward-Perkins, 1950: 93, chart 3).[10]

Early twentieth-century United States

In the late 1920s, enthusiastic stock speculation in the rapidly growing communications, automobile, transportation, chemical and utilities industries emerged, encouraged by the promise of rising living standards based on the new technological advances. The New York Stock Exchange saw an average annual increase in the neighbourhood of 21 to 28 per cent in the period 1926–1929 – from a low in 1923 to its peak in the autumn of 1929, the total increase was in excess of 330 per cent. New common stock issues rose by almost 660 per cent in half that time, and stock prices in the innovating industries increased by more than 200 per cent in three short years.

The speculation was driven more by recent successes and less, if at all, by future estimates of the fundamental earnings potential of a company, which could be seen in both the decline in capitalisation rates and the spectacular increase in both the quantity and value of investment trusts – an early form of the modern-day mutual fund. From 1921 through to 1926, 139 trusts with a portfolio value of $1 billion had been organised. By the fall of 1929, 770 trusts with a portfolio value exceeding $7 billion dollars existed (Carosso, 1970). In many cases, the portfolios of the newer trusts were not public information, and post-crash investigations revealed a significant degree of inter-trust pyramiding of sales.

Detailed evidence of participants in the speculation suggests that it remained largely limited to professional speculators. Only about 11 per cent of the speculators were not customers of member firms of the New York Stock Exchange (Carosso, 1970: 238–239). Despite the relatively small proportion of non-professionals, 'the striking thing about the stock market speculation of 1929 was not the massiveness of the participation. Rather, it was the way it became central to the culture' (Galbraith, 1955: 78).

In early September of 1929, news of a summer slowdown was released. A decline in manufacturing production and construction expenditures compounded problems emerging in the agricultural sector. The great bull market came to an end on September 3 and 'never again did the market manifest its old confidence. The later peaks were not peaks but brief interruptions of a downward trend' (Galbraith 1955: 83). By all accounts of the period, however, there was no warning of the extent of the crash or the severity of the depression (see, for example, Galbraith, 1955; Carosso, 1970; Temin, 1976).

The stock market crash in October of 1929 initiated a thirty-month decline in stock prices that eventually wiped out 80 per cent of the peak equity value and with it millions of dollars of paper wealth. Falling bond prices formed a major source of bank losses (see Friedman and Schwartz, 1963: 355–356). A wave of bank failures hit the nation between November of 1930 and March of 1933 when the President declared a National Bank holiday to stem the panic. Total bank deposits dropped by one-third, the volume of bank credit shrunk to 62 per cent of its 1929 level. Banks, struggling to maintain liquidity, sold off their portfolio of securities depressing market values – and the market value of remaining bank assets – further (Viner, 1936; Board of Governors of the Federal Reserve System, 1943; Friedman and Schwartz, 1963). An early economic recovery in the first few months of 1931 was aborted when the failure of the Creditanstalt bank in

Austria precipitated an international scramble for liquidity (Kindleberger, 1989). American banks found their reserves – already substantially depleted from an internal demand for currency – drained further by a rush for gold exports (Einzig, 1932; Friedman and Schwartz, 1963: 318).[11] By 1932–1933, more than 40 per cent of the 25,000 banks had failed, manufacturing output had dropped to a little more than half of its 1929 level, national income had declined by as much as one-third and one-quarter to one-third of the labour force was unemployed.

Late twentieth-century United States

In the 1980s, technological advance was radically altering the manner in which people communicated and managed information. By the early 1990s, the personal computer was fast becoming required equipment for businesses and, later on, for households. By 1997, the Internet – as a means of accessing a large and ever-increasing amount of information – was familiar to many. From 1995 through to 1999, American real gross domestic product (GDP) rose at a rate of 4 per cent annually, driven by a total fourfold increase in business investment in computers and related equipment. Companies at the heart of the advance as listed on the NASDAQ saw the index of their stock prices climb from a low of 600 in 1996 to a peak of more than 5000 in March of 2000. Nine months later, the index had dropped to under 2300, wiping out nearly $5 trillion of paper wealth before sinking to a low of 800 in the late summer of 2002. By comparison, the Wilshire 5000 Price Index – the broadest index of American share prices – declined by 26 per cent over the same period.

The NASDAQ market crash devastated the 'new economy' sector, venture capital dried up, banks experienced a sharp rise in loan losses and the rate of business investment declined, turning negative a year later. GDP growth dropped from an inflation-adjusted rate of 3.7 per cent in the first half of 2000 to 0.9 per cent in the second half. Employment slumped with a severe and sustained decline occurring in manufacturing. The economy entered a brief but severe recession in March of 2001 that ended nine months later, leaving the real GDP growth at a mere 0.3 per cent for that year (Bennett, 2003).

Late twentieth-century Thailand

From the mid-1980s onward, the rapid industrialisation and commercialisation of the Thai economy propelled Thailand forward in manner unmatched by that of the European, Japanese or American economies at the time. In 1990–1993, Thailand undertook a host of financial reforms designed to encourage foreign lending and portfolio investment. Thai authorities removed restrictions on currency convertability, created an offshore banking facility and removed stock market rules prohibiting foreign purchases of Thai equity. Japanese and Western financial firms attracted to the relatively high rates of returns in Thailand, and repelled by relatively low rates of return at home, 'generated a faddish enthusiasm' for Thailand as an 'emerging market' and 'Asian miracle'. With the Thai currency pegged to the US dollar and, more often, loans negotiated in foreign currencies, the currency risk of such investment was minimal. The surge in financial inflows headed principally for the banks and arrived in the form of short-term bank loans.

The economy quickly overheated with foreign debt reaching dangerous heights. Capital inflows fed inflation, the Thai baht became overvalued, Thai products lost their international competitiveness and Thailand's balance of payments deficit increased to nearly half of its GDP. Over investment in domestic infrastructure, heavy upstream industries and real estate generated overcapacity and falling returns. By 1995, returns on real estate were falling and the debt default of the property firms threatened the solvency of the finance industry. International speculation turned from lending on Thai development projects to undercutting the currency (Phongpaichit and Baker, 2000: 2–3).[12]

Unable to defend the attack, the baht was floated on 2 July 1997. In less than twelve months, the currency had lost half its value, wiping out Thai financial equity denominated in foreign currency. Net private capital outflows were equivalent to nearly one-fifth of Thailand's GDP, credit contracted, liquidity evaporated, production dropped, unemployment rose and the economy 'tipped into a headlong downward spiral that continued unabated for eighteen months' (Phongpaichit and Baker, 2000: 2–3). The crisis hit every sector of the economy, and from the summer of 1997 through to the fourth quarter of 1998, real GDP continued its decline to one-fifth of its peak two years earlier. The construction industry did not begin to recover until the third quarter of 1999, and the finance industry was still contracting by the end of that same year. While all suffered – with the incomes of a large number of people dropping below the poverty line – hardest hit were those at the top and bottom of the income scale, the poorly educated, and those in the rural northeast (the major source of city migrants) (Phongpaichit and Baker, 2000: 95).

Observations

In each episode, the preceding speculation centered on assets associated with an innovation that had some measure of economic and social importance. In most cases the innovation had a technological foundation. Advances in steam power led to railway development in England in the 1840s, which radically altered industrial growth and population location. Advances in communication and transportation industries in the 1920s were noticeably affecting the lifestyles of many in the United States, with communication and information technologies once again leading advances in the 1990s. Yet not all innovations were purely or even primarily technological at their core. Some were financial and had strong political overtones. In 1720, following John Law's experiment in Paris, England's parliament partnered with the South Sea Company to undertake a substantial debt for equity swap – a novel plan to reduce the burden of the state debt while, at the same time, introducing the possibility of acquiring wealth by means other than patrimony. In 1825, the need for specie and the desire to promote and support new notions of 'democracy' captivated for a brief time, the imaginations of many. In Thailand in the 1990s, the opening up of financial markets to international investors encouraged rapid economic and social change.

Four of the six episodes described here proceeded via purchases of share or equity ownership in the firms central to the adoption and distribution of the innovation and all episodes saw a significant expansion of credit supporting the speculation. Each crisis directly or indirectly recoiled from the previous speculation, and each episode involved a crisis of credit. Yet not all the crises were equally devastating. While the United States in the 1930s and Thailand in the late 1990s saw deep and widespread economic and social hardship, the crises of 1720 and 2000 were more contained and less severe. What explains these similarities? What explains the differences? This study explores these questions.

3 Capitalism

A culture of accumulation as the context for innovation

The purpose of this chapter is to sketch those aspects of capitalism that serve to locate the crisis within a set of socio-economic relations that shape and reinforce speculative behaviour. The process of innovation and accumulation as the driving force of capitalism, offers the individual the opportunity to speculate and defines the focus of his or her speculative activity. The culture of capitalism provides an explanation of the dominant values that motivate the speculator. Motivated to accumulate and innovate by the promise of material enrichment, the individual becomes part of a process that is inherently unstable at its core in the sense that the process of innovation and accumulation – in a Schumpeterian manner – drives the fluctuations in the level of business activity over time.

Capitalism and culture

Financial crises are foremost a capitalist phenomenon, for it is in the capitalist society alone that speculating on material advance occurs. Max Weber (1992 [1904]) conceives and articulates capitalism as a form of socio-economic organisation consisting of four basic features: the private ownership of resources, the pursuit of profit, freedom of interference from others and competition. These four basic features interact with a culture that values material wealth to create the capitalist imperative of material advance. The private ownership of resources permits the individual accrual of material reward. Where monetary values in exchange come to replace the use-value in activity, the pursuit of material reward translates into the pursuit of profit. The freedom of interference from others – what Isaiah Berlin (1969) identified as negative liberty – promotes the belief that individuals develop self-identity (based on individual wealth) independently of others. Freedom from interference – essentially the freedom of contract – is the freedom of mobility in employment and the freedom of individual consumption choice that promotes a belief of self-determination. Finally, the feature of competition both among consumers and between producers further advances the notion that material success is exclusively and rightfully the reward of individual achievement.

Material success, through the interpretive influence of the Protestant Ethic, is the metric for a strong ethical valuation of human effort and moral worth. The logic is simple. Moral people work hard and avoid sloth; people who work hard earn more income and accumulate more wealth. In the absence of any easier means of establishing and assessing one's true moral worth, one's relative material wealth serves as the proxy for relative moral worth. As Herbert McCloskey and John Zaller (1984) suggest, the Protestant Ethic provides a justification for the unequal distribution of income and wealth – knowing that not all are of equal honour morally justifies the disproportionate allocation of income and wealth to those more honourable.[1] Thus, material wealth has come to be identified with such substantive human characteristics as intelligence and industry. As John Galbraith (1990: 13–14) states:

> In all free-enterprise (once called capitalist) attitudes there is a strong tendency to believe that the more money,... of which an individual is possessed or with which he is associated, the deeper and more compelling his economic and social perception, the more astute and penetrating his mental processes. Money is the measure of capitalist achievement. The more money, the greater the achievement and the intelligence that supports it.

A 'reverence for the possession of money', the imputation of substantive value to things monetary, is a peculiar inversion of the problem of money as addressed by Georg Simmel a century ago. Considering in careful detail the limitations and implications of objectifying relationships and converting them into monetary value, Simmel (1990 [1907]: 404) concluded that the 'money value of things does not fully replace what we ourselves possess in them, that they have qualities not expressed by money'. The eighteenth-century conversion into money of land owned by the German peasant could not fully compensate for the purpose and fulfilment that owning the land itself offered.

> To the peasant, the land meant something altogether different from a mere property value; for him it meant the possibility of useful activity, a centre of interest, a value that determined his life, which he lost as soon as he owned only the money value of his land instead of the land itself.
>
> (Simmel, 1990 [1907]: 399)

The rendering into a commodity the effort of one's labour entails the same loss, as Karl Marx (1971 [1859]) and Simmel have both argued. To impute to money and wealth substantive value is to engage in a process of regaining or recouping this loss of life – contents or life purpose – the source of genuine life fulfilment. The substitution of quantifiable abstract forms of purchasing power can never fully replace, however, the value one derives from qualitative relationships.

The desire to broadcast one's worth stems from the innate desire of the individual to belong in the social. Confronting and contradicting the privileged ethos of possessive individualism, the desire to belong creates a tension that frustrates fulfilment. In open and differentiated societies, status confers both a sense of belonging and a sense of individual importance – a manifestation of Simmel's (1957) 'dualistic nature'. The combination of the social and human importance conferred upon monetary wealth together with its unequal distribution defines a differentiated society. Where the society is more complex such that associations of persons are loose and distant, the communication of one's social status relies on the accepted means of expressing differential status. Simmel, Thorstein Veblen (1912) and others maintain that the typical means of communication entail the social display of consumption.

Consumption afforded by one's income becomes the means by which one communicates one's relative material wealth and, hence, consumption becomes the means through which the individual socially validates her or his high moral significance. In the process of communicating individual achievement, material consumption becomes both a product of socialisation and the imperative of the economic order. Yet the possession and consumption of material goods to satisfy our need for social validation in an environment that is characteristically competitive can never fulfil such needs as the spiritual and emotional. Perpetually striving to consume more, individuals with unfulfilled desires ensure the continuing need to accumulate, and thus ensure the reproduction of the capitalist order. As Zygmunt Bauman (1987) states (as quoted in Giddens, 1991: 198):

> Individual needs of personal autonomy, self-definition, authentic life or personal perfection are all translated into the need to possess, and consume, market-offered goods. This translation, however, pertains to the appearance of use value of such goods, rather than to the use value itself; as such, it is intrinsically inadequate and ultimately self-defeating, leading to momentary assuagement of desires and lasting frustration of needs.... The gap between human needs and individual desires is produced by market domination; this gap is, at the same time, a condition of its reproduction. The market feeds on the unhappiness it generates: the fears, anxieties and the sufferings of personal inadequacy it induces release the consumer behaviour indispensable to its continuation.

The desire to possess goods for consumption as a means of filling the void in self-fulfilment that is left by the process of commodifying that in turn alienates labour, becomes, as Anthony Giddens maintains, a substitute for the 'genuine development of self'. Max Horkheimer and Theodor Adorno (1982) consider the possibility that alienation is the outcome of a process of externalising what is internal to the subject thus impoverishing the subject. Fundamentally impoverished, the desire to consume is insatiable. This insatiable desire to consume an ever-increasing or ever-novel basket of goods ensures, in turn, that accumulation and expansion can continue. In this way, the desire to accumulate material wealth becomes the focus of the capitalist production system. Expansion becomes an imperative with innovation its driving force.

Capitalism as a process of innovation

With capitalism driven by the need to accumulate and human desires only temporarily fulfilled by the consumption of market-offered goods, the need to innovate becomes paramount. The essence of capitalism as an economic process lies in its continual adaptation to innovation and its perpetual reconfiguring of the matrix of the inputs of land, labour and physical capital and the outputs in the production of services and material goods. As the primary process underlying the ebb and flow of business activity, innovation forms the basis of an instability that, when later layered with the institutional features characteristic of finance capitalism, creates an environment prone to crisis.[2]

Innovation is borne of invention, though the two activities are quite distinct. Invention is mechanical or scientific; it is the development of new products or the creation of new technologies, for example, whether or not involving systematic knowledge. Innovation is primarily economic. It is the action of Joseph Schumpeter's (1939) innovators and Alfred Chandler's (1990) pioneers and first movers – the entrepreneurs who first bring the invention into commercial use and who make the investments in production, distribution and management necessary to achieve competitive advantage in the new product or process. Yet conceptually confining the definition of an innovation to the 'setting up of a new production function', as Schumpeter does, obscures essential elements. Production functions and their cost counterparts restrict the problem too narrowly. Traditional economic representations of production focus on one-to-one mappings of inputs to outputs. These representations inadequately accommodate joint products and economies of scope. Simple production functions capture nothing of the dramatic transformational potential of some innovations and detrimentally obscure key developments in modern industrial and financial capitalism.

To be sure, a new production function may capture well the impact of some innovations but this will not always be the case. It is advantageous to differentiate those innovations well represented by a realignment of the relationship between inputs and outputs from those innovations that have the power to transform the organisation of the entire economy (or much of it), and with it society's very culture. Adapting Seabury Gilfillan's (1967 [1935]) taxonomy, as adopted by Donald Cardwell (1995), we may differentiate here between innovations that are evolutionary and innovations that are revolutionary.[3]

Evolutionary innovations are represented reasonably well by either a shift of an existing production function in the same input–output space or by a new production function in the old (new) input but new (old) output space. Evolutionary innovations stem from evolutionary inventions – changes that are in the nature of a piecemeal accumulation of knowledge resulting in incremental improvements in the basic design. Evolutionary improvements (both invention and innovation) tend to be changes that come from within an existing industrial structure, that adapt a pre-existing technology, are advanced by persons inside the industry and easily recognised and adopted by the existing authority structures. The opportunity for evolutionary innovation to impact noticeably on industries and processes that are not directly connected to the first industry affected is limited. Because the impact is contained both in the sense of affecting only (or primarily) the one industry, being theoretically contained in the same production space, the impact of an innovation on output, costs and revenues may be reasonably predicted.

Revolutionary inventions and innovations contrast conceptually with evolutionary improvements. Revolutionary inventions are first associated with either a wholly new technology or a radically altered form of some pre-existing technology. Whichever or however interpreted, these changes are revolutionary in the sense that they have the capability of creating a new industry and significantly transforming existing industries in ways that affect otherwise unrelated spheres of economic activity. Revolutionary innovations – as with revolutionary inventions – typically come from outside the existing authority structures, and are introduced by pioneers unrelated to the industries first affected. Revolutionary innovations demonstrate the ability to radically alter the manner in which the economy and the society are organised. Conversely, radically new techniques 'cannot be introduced without changes in social relations; it is at the same time the possibility and the wish to introduce new techniques that encourages changes in social relations' (Cohen, 1978: 50). In other words, revolutionary innovations are transformative in character. Because of the transformative power of the revolutionary innovation, any fundamental impact must be uncertain in the early stages of adoption.

In terms of economic impact, revolutionary innovations change the process by which information flow or production is organised and supported, or both. Such fundamental changes affect the costs of many industries, transforming in new and unpredictable ways the economy's matrix of relative prices. Radically altered cost advantages spur, in turn, widespread industrial restructuring. In other words, the importance of the revolutionary innovation does not stop – by virtue of its transformative potential – with any first impact. Instead, the innovation continues to spawn further developments for many years. The diffusion process involves a considerable number of feedback loops wherein both technological advance and organisational restructuring enhance and are enhanced by the changing manner in which information flows and the economy is organised. In short, the impact of a revolutionary innovation is cumulative, self-sustaining and ultimately universal in impact. As Nathan Rosenberg (1994: 15) states:

> A [revolutionary] innovation is one that provides a framework for a large number of subsequent innovations, each of which is dependent upon, or complementary to, the original one.... [E]ach constitutes the initiation of a long sequence of path-dependent activities, typically extending over several decades, in which later developments cannot be understood except as part of a historical sequence.

The time lag between the initial invention that later proves revolutionary and the innovation it sparks may be substantial. James Watt's patent on the first steam engine preceded England's railway boom of the1840s by some seventy years. A similar boom in the United States was delayed by an additional ten or so years. In 1896, Guglielmo Marconi patented the first wireless telegraphy, but it was not until the 1920s that the radio was familiar to many, with the contemporaneous innovations of the television and the automobile sharing a similar temporal history. As one final example, although the universal computer had its origins in the early 1940s computational aids, it was not until the idea had evolved into a machine for personal use in the 1980s that the most recent of revolutionary innovations in information communications began.[4]

Rosenberg (1976, 1994) explores the factors influencing the diffusion of a revolutionary innovation. He explains the protracted adoption and adaptation of a given technological invention by economic and institutional constraints. In each of the earlier examples, as with all revolutionary innovations, by definition, there is an invention that gradually (matched with advances in the necessary supporting technologies) becomes commercially viable as an industrial product that is largely limited to aiding industrial production. It then evolves through further refinements into a product of luxury service value to the wealthy. For those products of technologies that evolve furthest to the point where the process of mass production can take advantage of unprecedented scale and scope economies, the potential for revolutionary impact is set.

The revolutionary innovation remains only a potential, however, until the industrial changes noticeably affect the lives of a large number of people otherwise unrelated to the industries from which the original invention sprouted. In other words, only once a product – previously foreign to the local culture – has gained widespread public appeal and has, in fact, transformed local culture by affecting the daily lives of a large proportion of the population is its revolutionary nature revealed.[5] The social adjustment and impact are subtle, difficult to reconstruct historically, and more difficult to predict or even identify clearly in contemporaneous periods. Yet, for its ability to influence the potential for financial instability, the diffusion of a revolutionary innovation is much more important.[6]

The diffusion process excites others to action. The early success of an innovation stimulates a 'bandwagon' effect that is critical to the diffusion process of a given innovation and that inspires innovations in peripheral industries and markets. In what is essentially Schumpeter's 'one-sided rushes' of firms jumping into a rapidly growing new branch of industry, 'the bandwagon effect is extraordinarily important.... [it] is a vivid metaphor and it relates to a rapid diffusion process which occurs when it becomes evident that the basic innovations can generate super-profits and may destroy older products and processes' (Freeman *et al.*, 1982: 67). Where a given innovation has the capacity to affect the operation of a large number of industries, the capacity for social change and contemporaneous innovations is high. The development of the railway network in England in the mid-1800s involved complementary innovations in mechanical engineering industries, iron and steel industries, and the capital markets in addition to the training of a skilled labour force and the creation of an urban 'working class'.

What complicates the uncertainty around the objective potential of a given innovation is the uncertainty surrounding the particular form it will take. The particular form adopted, in turn, defines the 'winners' in the race to gain market dominance. In an outline of the history of the automobile industry in Europe and the United States, Burton Klein (1977) demonstrates that, in the initial stages of development, it was by no means clear that the American-produced internal combustion engine would emerge the leader. In the early stages, European innovation was leading American and in 1900, it was the steam and electric vehicles that accounted for three-fourths of the total output of vehicles by American firms. It was not until Ford introduced the radical organisational innovation of assembly line production that the historical place of the internal combustion engine and the gasoline-powered vehicle was secured and the path of future transportation development was set. The path of more recent developments in information and communications technologies shares a similar history.

While the initial struggle for dominance leaves the potential for success wide open, '[o]nce a development path is set on a particular course, the network externalities, the learning process of organizations, and the historically derived subjective modeling of the issues reinforce the course' (Douglass North, 1990: 99). Large set-up costs, learning effects and coordination effects create self-reinforcing mechanisms that ensure a given path will be followed (see Arthur, 1988). Yet we cannot judge the path dominated by any one outcome as more efficient than that which would have been defined by some competitive alternative – we cannot say that the gasoline powered engine is or was a more efficient path than that which would have been defined by the dominance of the steam powered or electricity powered automobile. What we can seek to discover in our attempt to better understand the source and evolution of financial instability are the linkages between the institutional structure and the economic behaviour (see Furubotn and Richter, 1991; Swedberg and Granovetter, 1992).

Implications for crises

The ebb and flow of business activity in the continual adaptation to innovation defines the primary source of instability inherent in the capitalist system.[7] Driven by the socially constructed need to accumulate wealth, innovation becomes the engine of expansion. Revolutionary innovations, by virtue of their wide-ranging potential effect on the social and economic lives of individuals, offer the greatest potential for speculative material gain and thus attract the most attention. Were this all that operated, the ebb and flow of business activity would simply be mirrored in a corresponding speculative enthusiasm that itself waxed and waned with the adoption of and adaptation to the latest innovation. Throughout its diffusion, however, the potential for a revolutionary innovation to generate material gain remains fundamentally uncertain. Such uncertainty opens the door to additional social influences. Over and above validating the individual's moral worth, the social assessment of potential gain informs and reinforces the individual's own assessment in a manner that can create and feed euphoria. Separately, an individual's desire to display publicly his or her material worth and hence moral value extends beyond consumption goods into the objects of the speculation itself. These two additional considerations combine to create conditions that are ripe for mass speculation in capitalist enterprise. Both the exaggeration of the prior speculation and the forces that permit it introduce the possibility that the inevitable downturn in business activity will degenerate into a crisis. In Chapters 4 and 5, I discuss each of these two complicating influences in turn.

4 The impact of uncertainty on (in)forming behaviour

Crises are essentially institutional phenomena occurring when institutions fail in their operations and fail in their role to reduce uncertainty. Institutions – as rules and conventions governing behaviour – impose a structure on social interaction, serving to reduce uncertainty by rendering behaviour predictable. Innovation, by initiating a shift in the social and economic landscape, reintroduces uncertainty and forces an adaptation of behaviour to the evolving environment. Throughout the initial stages of diffusion, speculation on the incalculable promise of the revolutionary innovation becomes increasingly tenuous and generates fertile ground for a crisis. In this way, both crises and institutions owe their core existence to the fact that we face a fundamental uncertainty about future circumstances; crises would not occur nor would institutions exist otherwise.

Uncertainty that escapes calculated predictions over possible future outcomes raises critical questions about how behaviour is motivated when information is incomplete and imperfect. When fundamental uncertainty reigns, we do not have objective estimates of potential outcomes to inform choice and action. The assumptions of traditional economic analysis are thus invalid and the analysis is of little use in grasping the issues at hand. Instead, it is through exploring the role institutions play in patterning behaviour that brings us a little closer to understanding both the speculative behaviour that precedes a crisis and the institutions that define the context.

As a first step towards a fuller understanding of the institutional context of crises, this chapter explores the process of decision-making. By highlighting the inapplicability of traditional economic treatments of the rational deliberative process to the study of this phenomenon, entertaining the limitations imposed by the unknown and considering the manner in which we operate in the uncertain environment, this chapter seeks to underscore the importance of uncertainty in explaining institutions and conventions as coping strategies.

Beyond understanding the need for institutions, the analysis of behaviour in the face of uncertainty plays a second yet equally important role in the analysis of crises. Revolutionary innovation, as an experiment never before tried, reintroduces uncertainty of a particular nature, erodes the previously constructed predictability and ultimately challenges the effectiveness of the old institutions. The innovation itself has the potential to offer material advance, but the extent and range of that advance remains fundamentally uncertain until much later in the diffusion process. The promise of material advance in a culture that is acquisitive and that values material wealth sparks an outburst of speculation as noted in Chapter 3. The optimism attached to potential gain cannot be and is not justified; however, by any rational calculations of possible outcomes. In default of a known future, speculative optimism becomes dependent on the collective assessment of that potential gain. It is in these periods of transition and advance when fashion, as a collective dynamic, has the potential to swamp the individual decision and renders institutions especially fragile.

Decisions and rational choice

There exists in all of us a desire to maintain some degree of clarity and predictability over ourselves and our environment. The presence of ambiguity and unpredictability will determine how people cope in different situations. Russell Fazio (1986) suggests that highly consequential behaviours, such as choosing a life partner or deciding which career to pursue, often invoke thoughtful deliberative analysis. The inconsequential daily behaviours may be spontaneous or determined by convention, habit or custom, and are often non-deliberative in nature. Yet the two may conflate. Convention – as understandings that organise and coordinate action in predictable ways – may inform the analysis applied to highly consequential behaviours; how and who decides whom one will marry might be determined by a custom summoned to decide this highly consequential action. An analysis of the custom informing seemingly inconsequential behaviours might suggest a 'rational' or reasoned justification for such accepted practices.

Information and the certainly rational

In taking a course of action, one must first decide to act deliberatively or to adopt custom or convention as a non-deliberative behaviour. In choosing deliberate action over custom, one must then decide the set of information upon which to deliberate. Paradoxically, perhaps, custom itself might inform how one decides which information to use. For example, it is customary for economists to restrict analysis of individual behaviour to a set of information that exclusively consists of the utility one derives from consuming goods and services purchased with the income one earns. Where individuals have coherent preferences over known future circumstances, it may be reasonable to adopt the customary behavioural assumption that rational agents act in a manner that reflects a cost–benefit analysis informing a maximally efficient course of action.

In the absence of full information about the consequences of an action, economists customarily assume a certain-like behaviour. Rational economic agents uniformly adopt a cost–benefit analysis of *expected* outcomes over ordered preferences to the same end. The expectations framework formally employed, however, is equivalent to certainty. If an agent's subjective probabilities map into the objective probabilities suggested by some formal model and if these objective probabilities are linear over a finitely defined set of potential outcomes, then agents can reasonably employ a calculus that renders the 'uncertain' future equivalent to a certain one.

Yet, when the ontological outcome is uniquely identifiable and relevant information appears in the form of a full set of either finitely defined, deterministic outcomes or probabilistic ones; the choice and decision embedded in the formal model of economic behaviour simplifies the problem to the point where really no choice exists at all. The outcome is tautological – the rational actor will choose it; not to choose it is to act irrationally and, in so doing, to violate the assumption of rationality. Assuming a dominance of rational actors ensures an equilibrium outcome (however defined) that is free of crises (as disequilibrium phenomena) and devoid of institutions.

Bounded rationality

The problem of decision-making becomes more interesting when we acknowledge limitations on the information available or the ability of rational actors to process the sheer amount of that information or both. Faced with the inability to completely and exhaustively comprehend, process or evaluate the raw data, (or some combination of the three limitations), individuals are thus unable to provide a comprehensive list of future outcomes and thus cannot clearly differentiate between alternative courses of action. Such limits on one's abilities introduce Herbert Simon's (1978) concept of 'bounded rationality' – a situation characterised as one in which the actor faces an epistemological uncertainty in an ontologically certain world. The world is potentially and eventually knowable; it is immutable and ergodic, if deterministically complex. The economy converges to a predetermined and socially efficient matrix of goods produced and consumed; but it takes a sequence of periods over which individuals 'discover' that outcome.

In such a complex environment, there exists the process of agents 'learning' the potentially knowable multifaceted, complicated environment in which they function. Observing, over a sequence of decisions, systematic errors in judgement – errors that could not have been observed in an earlier period – the behaviour may evolve in convergent fashion to the maximally efficient behaviour identified in the certain-equivalent environment. Surprises diminish as one eventually learns objective probability distributions of eventual outcomes. In this environment, the problem of computation is confronted with what Herbert Simon (1978) defines as procedural rationality, or that rationality of a person from whom computation is the scarce resource. Here, rationality applies to the ability to adapt successfully to emerging situations, determined by the efficiency of the decision-making and problem-solving processes. Omar Hamouda and Robin Rowley (1988: 85, emphasis added) contrast Simon's notion of procedural rationality, which stresses the effectiveness of the procedures used to *choose* actions, given cognitive and computational limitations, with a substantive rationality, which 'deals with the extent to which appropriate courses of action are *chosen*' and which best describes economists' notion of 'rational' in non-complex systems.

Complex worlds and institutions

Institutions emerge in a complex environment for two related reasons. Where information is limited and difficult to process, institutions as conventions ease the difficulty of decision-making. Where the process of exchange is costly, institutions provide a means of reducing the time and other resources required to negotiate the exchange. Were the world static, we could conceive of the evolution of bounded rational outcomes as approaching the completely rational outcome of traditional economics. In the 'long run' in such a world, however, institutions would lose their justification (see Dunn, 2000, 2001).

The environment under capitalism is not static, however. True uncertainty derives from both the absence of information about future prospects and from the presence of different abilities to comprehend that information which is available. Facing uncertainty, the decision problem may be difficult. Substantive rational assessments cannot be made, and the implications for procedural rationality of this environment is unclear (see Samuelson, 2004). The gap between the competence to understand the environment and the difficulty of the decision problems faced explains what Ronald Heiner terms the 'decision-competence' gap. Heiner (1983: 585) demonstrates that 'uncertainty is the basic source of predictable behavior, and also the main conditioning factor of evolutionary processes through which such behavior evolves. Uncertainty exists because agents cannot decipher all of the complexity of the decision problem they face, which literally prevents them from selecting most preferred alternatives'. The decision-competence gap explains the origins of predictable behaviour, where institutions – as setting rules and codes of conduct – emerge as the means by which to structure social interaction in an environment of uncertainty that is born of procedural complexity.

When information is costly and the actions of many require coordination, it is cost-efficient to self-impose institutions as the structure for and constraints on behaviour; that is, to create and impose the 'rules of the game'. The costs of transacting derive from both the need to communicate and verify information about the goods and services exchanged and the need to define and enforce the property rights to those goods. As Douglass North (1990: 28) states: 'The total costs of production consist of the resource inputs of land, labor, and capital involved both in transforming the physical attributes of a good…and in transacting – defining, protecting, and enforcing the property rights to goods (the right to use, the right to derive income from the use of, the right to exclude, and the right to exchange).'

Institutions emerge as a means of reducing these transactions costs. For example, standard contracts facilitate economic exchange because they are supported by a set of economic rules defining property rights and they are enforceable by a corresponding set of legal rules enforcing the claim on goods. By reducing the time to gather and assess relevant information, institutions reduce transactions costs by improving access and processing of the necessary information.

In complex societies, with a corresponding complexity to exchange, the institutions necessary to accomplish this objective of reducing transactions costs become themselves increasingly complex.

> The institutions necessary to accomplish economic exchange vary in their complexity, from those that solve simple exchange problems to ones that extend across space and time and numerous individuals. The degree of complexity in economic exchange is a function of the level of contracts necessary to undertake exchange in economies of various degrees of specialization.…The greater the specialization and the number and variability of valuable attributes, the more weight must be put on reliable institutions that allow individuals to engage in complex contracting with a minimum of uncertainty about whether the terms of the contract can be realized.
>
> (North, 1990: 34)

Institutions may be informal conventions or formally codified rules. The extent to which a society adopts formal institutions over informal ones will itself be a function of the degree of complexity in exchange. With increasingly complex trades, the benefits of standardising contracts and developing enterprises devoted to mediating the ultimate trades, for example, appear in the form of lower transactions costs and thus gain from formalising the transactions. As North (1990: 46) elaborates,

> The increasing complexity of societies would naturally raise the rate of return to the formalization of constraints.... The creation of formal legal systems to handle more complex disputes entails formal rules; hierarchies that evolve with more complex organization entail formal structures to specify principal/agent relationships.

Interdependencies and intersubjectivities

Both formal rational or bounded rational choice models assume that independent individual preferences are paired with immutable (eventually) identifiable maximal outcomes. Pervasive in economics and to a lesser degree in other social sciences is the belief of the individual as the explanatory primitive. The environments described by and assumed in the customary economic models of public choice and positive political economy do not accommodate the complex dynamics introduced by social or economic interaction and feedback (see Davidson, 1996, 1982–1983). If preferences and needs are socially constituted, the meanings and interpretations of narratives are dependent on others and are thus irreducibly social and historical. The complexity of social interaction among heterogeneous agents may not unfold into a uniquely identifiable, maximally efficient outcome that is independent of the course of action chosen by any given group of individuals. John Maynard Keynes (1973a [1936]) describes this simply with his recounting of the indeterminateness with which one can pick the winner of a beauty contest.[1] Similarly, the decision to allocate a portfolio of assets across different employment possibilities yields a multiple of outcomes, each outcome dependent on the particular asset allocation decided. The intrusion of public opinion, the potential for strategic behaviour, the non-uniqueness of outcomes and dependence of outcomes on chosen courses of action suggest we face a world that is not merely complex but complex around a multiplicity of legitimate outcomes, none of which is uniquely maximally efficient.

The French Conventions School seeks to examine just what is a rational course of action when agents face uncertainty – when agents cannot assign probabilities to the consequences of their actions, when they cannot rank their preferences and when interpretations are debatable. Where and how do individuals find the social and psychological affirmation that as members of the group they need? Nicole Biggart and Thomas Beamish (2003: 456) summarise the approach.

> Conventions theorists find economic coordination to be a concern of rational individuals who achieve it via obedience to rules, norms, and intersubjectively mediated action of various forms ...[constructing] courses of action that are intersubjectively defensible and sustainable as economically rational acts.

Rationality, then, becomes an 'emergent, interpretive, and performance process' rather than an objectively calculating exercise assumed by the substantive rationality of actors.[2]

When faced with true uncertainty, the experiments conducted by Daniel Ellsberg (1961) suggest that agents will prefer definite to indefinite information; this suggests, in turn, a scope for creating the definite to remove the indefinite. When the problem of choice and decision-making is real, when complex situations hamper cognition and a host of outcomes are justifiable, people nevertheless desire to replace the indefinite with the definite; they have a need to resolve the uncertainty and restore clarity and predictability. In the absence of objective future information on which to deliberate, people will default to that which they know or believe. People will construct courses of action that others in the group sanction as acceptable and defensible. In the modern 'enlightened' world, it is the *performance* of rationality embedded in convention that is chosen as a routine approach to repetitive situations. The motivation is not cost savings. Rather, the motivation is to appear to others to be acting rationally and comes from the combination of the individual's desire to reduce the anxiety created by the uncertainty and to preserve (or to enhance) the individual's status in her or his social group.

If the application of deductive reasoning, assumed in a certain or near-certain world, fails for want of the raw data or the ability to process complex data then humans tend to rely on characteristic and predictable methods of inductive reasoning by seeking patterns and constructing temporary internal models with which to work. Experience, what has worked in the past, and the opinions of others will now inform the initial model that, in turn, informs decision and guides action. John Maynard Keynes (1973b [1937]: 114, with original emphasis) states:

> (1) We assume that the present is a much more serviceable guide to the future than a candid examination of past experience would show it to have been hitherto. In other words we largely ignore the prospect of future changes about the actual character of which we know nothing.

(2) We assume the *existing* state of opinion as expressed in prices and the character of existing output is based on a *correct* summing up of future prospects, so that we can accept it as such unless and until something new and relevant comes into the picture.
(3) Knowing that our own individual judgement is worthless, we endeavour to fall back on the judgement of the rest of the world which is perhaps better informed. That is, we endeavour to conform with the behaviour of the majority or the average. The psychology of a society of individuals each of whom is endeavouring to copy the others leads to what we may strictly term *conventional* judgement.

Subsequent experience and social interaction continually test impressions and patterns defined by internal models. If successful, initial actions reinforce the belief in the appropriateness of the impression previously formed and spur increasingly courageous action. In a manner similar to the emergent norm theory of Ralph Turner and Lewis Killian (1987), and supported by modern psychological research, Brian Arthur (1994: 407) explains, 'As feedback from the environment comes in, we may strengthen or weaken our beliefs in our current hypotheses, discarding some when they cease to perform, and replacing them as needed with new ones.'

In cases where conventional judgement informs the individual's assessment of future prospects *and* the individual desires *to appear to others* to be acting rationally, outcomes cannot be uniquely pre-determined by any independent estimate of costs and benefits. Rather, the particular matrix of institutions that emerge will now depend critically on the social. This explains why the particular institutional structure in capitalist economies varies from society to society despite the fact that the varieties of institutions execute the same basic functions.

Coping with revolutionary change

In addition to the consideration of a coping strategy defined by a type of inductive, socially defined, rationality that explains institutions as emerging convention, the differential abilities to process information transforms into the actions of leaders and followers. The leaders will be those who, by virtue of reputation or power or both, rely on models that in normal times better explain the environment and thus more accurately guide behaviour. If beliefs and internal models are unobservable, then others would only observe the increased incidence of (temporarily) fulfilled expectations and become followers of a fashion in the behavioural example set by the leaders. If the models informing leadership action are themselves complex, then discerning patterns of behaviour would remain out of reach to the followers. This decision-competence gap for leaders is reasonably smaller than that which amateurs and non-participants face in normal times.

The decision-competence gap, which so clearly differentiates leaders and followers in normal times, narrows significantly when adapting to a revolutionary change. The introduction and gradual diffusion of a revolutionary change challenges one's traditional ways of thinking and one's managing of day-to-day life. It is a change that transforms the economy and society and, for a growing number of people, erodes the security they derived from their certainty in the old rules and traditions. In the earlier stages of the diffusion of revolutionary change, there is a growing fundamental uncertainty that perforce moves people outside the established institutional patterns and structures; and with it, undermines the ability of the leaders to apply their relatively sophisticated internal models.

The previously stable environment, complex in its multitude of justifiable outcomes dependent on which leaders dominated, begins to change in novel ways. There can be no valid basis on which to classify this original circumstance. There is no internal model that will produce superior performance. Faced with such uncertainty, leaders now face the same degree of uncertainty that, for sake of exposition, has always confronted the followers. What initiates the investment in a revolutionary innovation? What stimulates the leaders to first speculate in it? In the environment described, with no basis on which to assess probabilities, it can only be the optimistic *belief* that there is a chance of material success and, with it, enhanced reputation. If we grant the internalised need to accumulate, the combination of an optimistic belief in advance, together with a need for it, incites action. In the first instance, it is and can only be a 'spontaneous urge to action' – Keynes's notion of 'animal spirits' (Keynes, 1973a [1936] VII: 161; see also Koppl, 1991). Initial success from this first move will prompt, in a reinforcing manner, further action. As the leaders rely increasingly on the same patterns and simple rule-governed behaviour as that of their followers – to the extent that leaders now rely on the past simply extrapolated to forecast the future – their behaviour becomes indistinguishable from the followers.

The simplified behaviour of the leader has the effect of rendering that behaviour more comprehensible to the followers at a time when attentions are increasingly focused on the widening impact of the innovation. Increased awareness of the innovation is concomitant with its widening impact and the uncertainty it has reintroduced.[3] Those affected by the innovation struggle to comprehend the unusual events surrounding them. Leaders remain leaders by convention and continue to offer by example a definite course of action – 'a positive suggestion in an ambivalent frame of reference'. They are the ones others turn to for first interpretations of the changes. As such, their role as leaders mutates into a role as 'keynoters' (Turner and Killian, 1987: 84). Thus, at a time when an increasing number of followers eagerly seek some interpretation of the changes that confront them, the message is simpler and so more easily understood.[4]

Fashion

With meanings socially constructed, there is no unique maximally efficient outcome defined deterministically by minimum costs independent of the social. In complex societies, with the association of persons loose, anonymous and distant, convention dialogically communicates an individual's status to the group in addition to communicating the group's accepted metrics of 'rationality' to the individual, thus offering the psychological affirmation needed. As Georg Simmel (1957), Thorstein Veblen (1912) and others demonstrate, the typical means of communicating one's self-importance and self-worth is through the display of material possessions. Where the distribution of material possessions offers a means of easily communicating differential status, the acquisition of such superficial displays of status becomes in itself a goal and invites imitation by those less fortunate. As Simmel (1957: 543) notes:

> Fashion is the imitation of a given example and satisfies the demand for social adaptation; it leads the individual upon the road which all travel, it furnishes a general condition, which resolves the conduct of every individual into a mere example....[F]ashion represents nothing more than one of the many forms of life by the aid of which we seek to combine the uniform spheres of activity the tendency towards social equalization with the desire for individual differentiation and change.

Yet displays of fashion need not be limited to consumption goods. When the objective is to display intelligence, industry and rationality, fashion will extend to the objects of speculation at those times when revolutionary advance commands the attention of an increasing number of people.

The introduction of such widespread novelty in an environment prone to 'fashion' creates the potential for a spreading enthusiasm. As with all fashion, it is a gradual swell of enthusiasm that is marked by the increasing participation of new and naïve participants who are motivated more by collective actions and less by any independent objective decision to participate. The geometric rate at which the speculative activity and excitement spreads is driven by the increased reliance on past successes, the increased pressure to appeal to others for affirmation of the appropriateness of one's actions and the self-fulfilling nature of the excitement.

Naïve followers are encouraged to participate. The increased public attention received by reported fashion captures the attentions of prior non-participants who are mentally calculating how much they would have gained when they first considered such participation. The success of an increasing number of persons with whom the prospective participant has some connection feeds the impression of feasibility and further encourages the taking of action. Ultimately, both social and economic gains attract new participants, the fear of diminished social status repels them from sitting any longer on the sidelines and the recent success of others makes them much less wary.

Fashion and its ritualistic imitation emerge; but they cannot continue forever. Eventually the opportunities for differentiating social status through displays of fashion are eliminated when the fashion becomes widely adopted by the masses. In those periods where it is fashionable to speculate on objects associated with a revolutionary innovation, the erosion of the opportunity for status differentiation might set a binding social limit to speculation. More likely, however, it will be the eventual revelation of the innovation's objective economic potential that will force the waning of all speculative enthusiasm.

The ideas put forth in this chapter paint a picture of a stable environment disturbed by an innovation. The focus here has been on the creation of institutions as the means by which we create the stable environment. Disturbed by an innovation, the initial effect is to generate heightened attention to the indefinite promise for material gain and spur speculation that shares many features in common with the phenomenon of fashion in material consumer goods. In the initial stages of diffusion, where future prospects must be unknown and unknowable, the optimism necessary to drive the speculation forward is assured by the self-fulfilling nature of the socially constituted meanings derivative of a desire to demonstrate one's social status. Such optimism is particularly and increasingly fragile due to the spreading imitation. While fashion in consumer goods may end with no material damage to the participants, the end of the fragile speculation risks loss of savings and future income. Any abrupt change in such a fragile environment will produce a panic. Mirroring the spread of the prior enthusiasm, the panic creates a social crisis. Mirroring the spread of the prior material advance, the panic creates a downward spiral of economic loss through the contraction of credit and the collapse of those institutions designed to exchange those funds in the capitalist economy.

In the second and third chapters, I have outlined key elements of the capitalist system necessary for understanding the context in which financial crises occur, and have explored the implications of uncertainty for behaviour in a stable environment that subsequently is disturbed by an innovation that forces behavioural adaptation. It is now necessary to look more closely at those institutions that form the basis of finance capitalism, generally, and periodic speculation, specifically, to ascertain the manner in which these institutional networks create the conditions for collapse and crisis. Only then will I be in a position to formulate a theory of financial crises that at once explains the similarities and provides a justification for the institutional sources of the differences.

5 Conventional approaches

Speculation as a fool's paradise

The institutions of finance in capitalist systems exist to transfer contracts that place claims on wealth. These institutions include a variety of products (currency, stocks, bonds and loan contracts), services (portfolio management and trustee services), markets (currency, equity and debt markets) and enterprises (retail and investment banks, insurance companies) designed to transfer purchasing power from those with excess funds to those in need of funds to finance current consumption and capital investment. When the institutions of finance themselves mediate the transfer of funds from the ultimate saver to the ultimate user of funds, within the system, the mediation process can be effected by either direct matching or indirect arrangement. The direct transfer of funds from the savers to the users of funds is executed by trading financial instruments in established markets. Alternatively, the ultimate transfer might pass through an intermediate financial enterprise, which becomes party to the transfer by signing contracts with the saver and, separately, with the user of the funds. The analysis of the process of intermediation and its role in the evolution of financial crises demands separate treatment, the analysis of which I reserve for a later chapter. In this and the next few chapters, I focus on the role financial instruments and enterprises play in the unfolding of an episode of instability.

The value of financial instruments

Financial instruments executing the transfer of funds are, in the capitalist economy, simply defined by the terms and conditions of the transfer of funds or purchasing power over time. As legal contracts in systems with well-defined property rights, the instruments are differentiated by such characteristics as the nature of the funds transfer (equity versus debt), the nature and amount of the income to be paid to the saver for the use of the funds, the denomination, primary issuer (corporation – financial or non-financial, government, individual) and the like. Standardised contracts, when paired with standardised accounting procedures, reduce transactions costs by rendering financial information readily accessible and easily decipherable. As such, the institutions of finance reduce uncertainty by systematising the process of measuring and exchanging claims to wealth.

In circumstances where real wealth includes the value of the underlying capital assets, then the contracts, directly or indirectly, are claims on the monetary value of these capital assets. Where the capital asset itself is indivisible, the institutional contracts are divisible and may be exchangeable. By establishing divisible contracts, the partitioning of an asset's total monetary value increases accessibility to savings and investment opportunities by requiring a smaller financial commitment. The ability to easily transfer title to these partial claims effectively enhances the liquidity of the underlying capital asset. Increased accessibility, together with increased liquidity, not only increase efficiency by ensuring that for a given exchange fewer resources are expended to transact it, but also encourage even greater savings, investment and accumulation and thus an even greater expansion of the capitalist system.

The existence of financial instruments as legal contracts that are available to transfer purchasing power over time has attracted a specialised interest in the determination of the prices of these instruments and the way in which the markets for them operates. As claims to underlying capital assets, it is unsurprising to find that the analysis of financial prices over time mirrors the formal analytics of the dynamic economy. The common analysis of portfolio allocation is conceptually identical to the economic analysis of the allocation of a fixed stock of resources across mutually exclusive opportunities to produce different capital goods.[1] Future profitability can be estimated and motivation is found exclusively in the self-interested desire to maximise wealth to create maximum consumption possibilities over time. Dynamic equilibrium is a series of static or momentary equilibria. Yet a fundamental indeterminacy exists in that there exist a multiple of equilibria satisfying the momentary conditions of the model, only a subset of which ensure convergence to a steady state with nothing internal to the model aiding the identification of the convergent choice. The remaining momentary equilibria place asset prices on a path to oblivion forever. In this narrow sense, the possibility that asset prices can deviate from that vector of prices consistent with a steady state captures elements of the 'speculative bubble', traditionally conceived as the result of self-fulfilling expectations of capital gains. In traditional finance perspectives on instability, the focus is on those technical issues that stem from the complexities introduced by the presence of a multitude of different financial instruments designed to mediate investment opportunities in a multitude of heterogeneous investment projects.

By examining briefly the conditions under which financial instability can arise in a world where the future is predictable and behaviour is independently motivated, the exercise highlights the rather unsatisfactory nature of the assumptions required to generate financial instability in this environment. In this way, the door is opened to exploring the importance of the assumption of true uncertainty and social and economic interdependence. As such, the exercise illustrates the limitations of the traditional view of financial instability and emphasises some of its critical elements that require further examination.

The conventional view of financial instability

In 1938, challenging the commonly held belief that 'a security is always worth what you can sell it for, no more and no less', John Burr Williams published his book entitled *The Theory of Investment Value*. In that book, Williams took one of the first appreciable steps towards a clear translation of the economic theories of interest and factor incomes into an evaluation of financial securities. Although bond tables were widely used by this time and therefore the notion of present value well established, formal analysis of financial securities values was just beginning. Williams, Irving Fisher (1930), Benjamin Graham and David Dodd (1934) each developed in this period, and with varying degrees of emphasis, the basic notion that securities prices or 'investment value' should be equal to the present worth of expected future income (dividends or coupons plus principal) generated by the security. This concept has since become the accepted definition of an asset's fundamental value – a value that defines, in turn, the value of the asset in a steady state.

> The most important single factor determining a stock's value is now held to be the *indicated average of future earning power*, i.e., the estimated average earnings for a future span of years. Intrinsic value would then be found by first forecasting this earning power and then multiplying that prediction by an appropriate "capitalization factor".
>
> (Graham *et al.*, 1962: 28, original emphasis)

The impact of this analysis, in combination with the introduction of laws such as the disclosure requirements of the 1930s, enhanced the quality of the information available and encouraged a collective focus on the fundamentals of securities investing. This encouragement has gone some distance to enhance the potential economic benefits of securities markets in the contemporary capitalist system. As investors focus more consciously on the future profitability of an asset, the possibility increases that asset markets could ensure an allocation of capital across alternative uses that yields maximum benefits, however the benefits are measured.

By the late 1950s, and early mid-1960s, the academic appeal of the concept of value investing was clear. In 1958, Franco Modigliani and Merton Miller extended the fundamental notion to transform the theory of optimal capital costs. Employing for very nearly the first time an arbitrage pricing argument to eliminate the compositional effects of financing costs, they showed that the market value of any firm is independent of its debt to equity ratio under certain assumptions. The Capital Asset Pricing Model, simultaneously developed by John Lintner (1965), Jan Mossin (1969) and William Sharpe (1964), demonstrated that under similar and similarly restrictive assumptions, equilibrium rates of return on risky assets were functionally related to the asset's covariance with the market portfolio. Risk-averse investors trading off risk against anticipated return chose current portfolios in a manner that yielded efficiency in equilibrium asset prices. In 1965, Eugene Fama published his influential work on the Efficient Markets Hypothesis, the essence of which asserts that individual asset prices will reflect fully and accurately the existing information that pertains to the income-earning potential of the asset. Combining all of these results and retaining similar assumptions, Joseph Stiglitz (1969, 1974) demonstrated that the value of the firm (asset) equals the value of the discounted cash flows from investment; any partition dividing the cash flows into risky debt and risky equity would have no impact on this value.[2]

Tractability and similar conveniences may explain the persistence of these and other simplifications. The orthodox models remain mechanical models that instrumentally are technical representations of complete and competitive markets in equilibrium. Such characterisations are justified by an appeal to the satisfaction gained from consumption (or profits as income to afford consumption) as the motivator of the agents' conduct. If agents are able to reason (and are hence rational), pleasure (pain) is solely the object of value (disvalue), and pleasure is derived only from consumption of goods, then we can conclude that agents must be acting in a way so as to maximise their own utility. If the set of objective data that inform these agents is imperfect, the relevant information set is assumed, nevertheless, to contain a complete and finite set of possible, contingent outcomes. For the individual, what must be an array of subjective contingent outcomes is assumed equal to the values, range and probabilities of the array of objective market outcomes by the researcher. To be in the possession of such information about market outcomes is, in conventional treatments, to know the true representation or model of the market. The orthodox theorist assumes that each individual market participant 'knows the market', that is, holds a justified true belief of what constitutes and influences the market prices of financial assets.

The implication of this traditional perspective of finance is the appealing notion that efficient capital markets produce equilibrium asset prices that reconcile marginal (risk-adjusted) rates of return for all savings and investments. As accurate signals, actual prices then can reliably guide rational capital allocation toward its most productive uses while inaccurate price signals, such as those suggested by the dynamically unstable growth paths, yield misallocation. The asset's fundamental value defines its steady state price; as such, a speculative bubble translates into asset prices driven up in excess of fundamental values and away from the steady state outcome. The troubling possibility of dynamic instability as it appears in the contemporary literature is now little more than the theoretical basis for debates about econometric signals. The debate all but exclusively centres on whether the observed volatility of measured indices of asset prices may be adequately explained in a formal statistical sense by any initiating volatility in the researcher's estimate of the underlying fundamentals. Indeed, the extent to which controversial debate stems from different beliefs among researchers belies the faith of all in accepting the homogeneity of rational investors.

Financing innovation – speculation in real assets

To underscore some of the essential limitations of the conventional perspective of financial market instability, consider the scenario wherein debt-financed investment in the assets of an evolutionary innovation. In the adjustment to evolutionary innovations, business fluctuations will be apparent in the uneven progress of capital accumulation, aided by institutionally supplied credit at relatively favourable market rates of interest in a cumulative process of the type analysed by Knut Wicksell (1936 [1898], 1978 [1935]). In the adoption and adaptation of an evolutionary innovation – by definition a risky but not uncertain venture – the range of possible future outcomes are reasonably known, an assumption consistent with the orthodox finance perspectives. In this situation, 'excess' speculation (of the type that generates extreme instability in the traditional models) can only exist on the introduction of the ignorant speculator and the ignorant lender. By highlighting the exclusive compatibility of the traditional view with adjustment to an evolutionary innovation and exposing its shortcomings as a reasonable explanation of instability in this environment, the door is opened to pursuing the importance of uncertainty in the face of a revolutionary innovation. To highlight the contention that financial instruments do more than simply reflect, in a neutral manner, the underlying dynamic problem that arises in the allocation of capital assets – as orthodox finance theorists suggest – the exercise is conducted under the assumption that speculation via financial instruments would be equivalent to speculation directly in the capital assets themselves. As a heuristic, this exercise is intended to motivate the importance of both uncertainty in the face of a revolutionary innovation and the fact that *something* in the conversion from intrinsic investment value of real capital to liquid marketable claims affects the assessed value of the corresponding financial instruments; points I will take up in the next chapter.

If speculation is limited to the acquisition of the relatively illiquid physical assets associated with an evolutionary innovation, speculators can reasonably assume that the losses from an adverse turn of events will be borne by themselves when these assets are relatively illiquid. Thus, speculators have every incentive to internalise the costs of the associated risk. Where the innovation promises greater productivity and a higher rate of return, access to loanable funds to finance the speculative investment becomes relatively more attractive for a given cost of credit.[3] Assuming a range of profitable outcomes with known probabilities, extending credit to a risky enterprise remains completely justified by forecasts of future profitability. If expectations of success are fulfilled, then the introduction of credit to finance the innovation usefully aided the reallocation of resources to the new endeavour. If expectations are disappointed, but were based solidly on an 'actuarial rationality' – that is, information about the true likelihood of alternative outcomes – distress will be limited. Debt obligations with now no profit from which to discharge that debt may result in default, but that risk was expected and hence properly priced under some basic assumptions about debt markets and risk calculations of institutional lenders. Although disappointed expectations may pose hardship for both the entrepreneur and the lender, it is reasonable to expect that the hardship will remain contained to the principals, spreading to unrelated businesses neither through asset channels nor through credit channels. In addition, because the fundamentals of the innovation are predictable and predicted, speculation and associate lending are rational in the sense that they are grounded in an objective forward estimate of future profits to the owner – speculators in real assets.

When the impulse to innovate is evolutionary in character, such an environment as the one just described exists. As incremental modifications located in a pre-existing industry, these innovations may reasonably have predictable, if only probable, profit outcomes. With fundamentals calculable, speculative excess requires the introduction of a speculator prepared to ignore them. In most explanations, this is the naïve speculator – an investor enamoured of recent past capital gains who, on this backward looking information alone, predicts future gains. By jumping into a rising market in sufficient numbers – buying an asset they expect will rise in price – the naïve speculators will find their naïve expectations temporarily fulfilled and the asset's price driven up beyond that which true expected fundamentals can justify. Disregarding or being ignorant of the true fundamentals, the naïve speculator embodies the wave of irrational exuberance that characterises the common notion of 'overtrading' in a 'bubble market'.

The introduction of the naïve speculator with access to loanable funds creates a potentially more hazardous situation. In the first instance, it appears that naïve speculation may, too, draw resources from otherwise productive employs through the mechanism of credit creation described briefly earlier. With a greater proportion of the economy's resources directed towards this naïve speculative activity – an activity that has a greater chance of failing than it does of succeeding – the recoil from this temporary prosperity will entail greater hardship for all participants.[4]

If one grants the possibility of debt-financed speculation, the implications for the consequent portfolio risk are clear. Institutional lenders who ignore information that directly affects the risk level of their capital investments do so at their own peril. Widespread wilful ignorance suggests risk improperly priced. The detrimental implications clearly follow. On the inevitable recession of the speculative optimism, there exists a greater probability of default on debt improperly priced and so a greater likelihood of creditor bankruptcy. Where the naïve creditor is a lender in other, otherwise unrelated, enterprises creditor bankruptcy will result in a contraction of credit greater than even the elimination of the innovation's relative profitability and its secondary naïve speculation would entail. Such an aggregate decline in credit below that level consistent with the new equilibrium will induce a temporary fall in output that is below its normal level.

For John Stuart Mill (1965 [1848]), Alfred Marshall (1923), Robert Flood and Peter Garber (1980), Bradford De Long *et al.* (1990) and a host of others, it is the activity of the naïve speculator – swept up in a wave of spontaneous optimism – that explains an excess doomed to collapse. In such a world, one must logically conclude that if only these naïve speculators knew better than to jump into what is essentially a pyramid scheme, there would be no bubble and no subsequent crisis on its collapse. That they do not know better leaves a theory of financial instability ultimately and solely attributable to excessive cyclical economic fluctuations caused by unjustified and unreasonable speculative behaviour.

The primacy of the naïve speculator must insufficiently explain the phenomenon, however. If credit is the primary means by which to finance speculation in innovative endeavours, this particular explanation of financial instability requires that there exist not only naïve speculators but naïve creditors as well. To the extent that institutions provide the channel through which the credit to finance naïve speculation in real assets passes, it becomes increasingly difficult to defend the assumptions of this explanation. Such an explanation requires more than simply naïve speculators; by including naïve creditors, it requires recourse to an assumption of widespread wilful blindness to the objective facts publicly available to and from industry experts. Consequently, we cannot be satisfied with this as a sole or even primary explanation of unstable and fragile financial markets. With evolutionary innovation – by definition coming from inside an existing industry – such possibilities of secondary or naïve speculation in the investment in *real* assets is unlikely. Naïve speculators who attempt to obtain credit for such activity will be approaching lenders who may reasonably be expected to have some connection with or access to industry experts. Through the lending channel, to the extent that the end use of loans is identified and identifiable, there exists a check in the system that can prevent credit-financed naïve speculation in real assets.

Many objective dimensions of the aforementioned analysis are important for understanding the threat of instability posed by debt-financed speculation. The interaction of credit and the accumulation process is foremost among them. Exploring these dimensions in the context of a scenario that limits speculation to the real assets associated with an evolutionary innovation underscores the inadequate nature of the assumptions about information and behaviour central to both traditional securities analyses and the common notion of a speculative bubble. In this scenario, if the traditional bubble is to occur, it can appear only when a host of experts in the innovating industry and credit industry ignore readily available and easily interpreted information and, in the formal version, will never burst. Naïve speculators, by definition ignorant of the objective potential of the speculative asset, nevertheless know that future losses, if any, will be inescapable by virtue of the relative illiquidity of the asset they acquire. In this scenario, all are jumping into a speculation that some know is objectively unjustifiable and all know any losses are their own. The assumptions required to legitimate the foregoing explanation of financial instability have come together to paint a rather disappointing picture of voluntary ignorance and irrationality. This reduction to a 'greater fool theory' of speculation and subsequent distress is, as many appreciate, a rather unsatisfactory explanation of events. Set out in this way, it should be apparent that to develop a fuller understanding of financial crises, we must explore the role of financial equities in enhancing the liquidity of the underlying capital assets and the manner in which institutionalized sources of credit encourage speculation in those innovations, the potential of which are not as easily defined.

Part II

The progression of a mania–panic episode

6 Justifications and means

The institutional organisation of speculation

Financial instability emerges from a very different environment than that described in Chapter 5. Financial instruments, and the enterprises that issue them, are more than simply a neutral means of mediating exchange between present and future consumption; they are the means in which opinion and sentiment affect real outcomes. Money is more than a medium of exchange and wealth is more than the discounted value of future income from which to consume. Money and wealth are also metrics for social status, intelligence and industry, yielding individual benefits that a focus on consumption alone cannot capture. Money and wealth are the motivators that can, at times, generate a fad behaviour that intoxicates all those desiring to climb the social ladders to success. In contrast, liquid equity claims on firms are less than the internal value of the firm, transforming incompletely into money value the total social and economic value of the firm's assets. Finally, banks are more than efficient intermediaries in the transfer of funds, diversifying risks and resolving the problems deriving from the existence of asymmetric information. Banks are part of a credit creation process that a widespread optimism can carry to seemingly unlimited heights.

While we all face a degree of true uncertainty at all times, at those times when we are confronted with an optimistic uncertainty as that created by some innovations of technological or institutional origin, socially determined waves of optimism afforded by an incalculable promise replaces the individual's forward estimates of profitability based on knowable outcomes with calculable probabilities. In the downturn, a debt-deflation spiral is a real threat precisely because the debt level of any one firm can affect the unit cost of debt service or the value of collateral assets potentially sold to repay debts or both. It is an environment, in other words, in which financial instability is conceived as a path-dependent process determined by dynamic market adjustments to disequilibria that are caused by large disturbances in uncertain environments. Markets are incomplete, investors are ill-informed and susceptible to fashionable pressures, the relevant streams of income and debt obligations can become mismatched, and the individual investments and investors are placed in the wider confines of aggregate economic and social developments rather than explicitly separated from them.

The purpose of this chapter is to examine the role played by financial equities in promoting speculative investment wherein the environment considered reflects these realities. The premise that divisible, liquid, claims on the monetary value of these capital assets reduces transactions costs and increases efficiency remains reasonable. Moreover, when standardised, these claims to wealth reduce uncertainty by systematising the process of measuring and exchanging them. Yet, importantly and paradoxically, this chapter explores the manner in which these institutions of finance capitalism also introduce ignorance. The process of converting money values externalises incompletely the qualitative values of both the tangible capital assets (such as machines, factories and inventories) and the intangible assets of knowledge (in the form of patents and trademarks). Furthermore, increased accessibility encourages participation by those less informed and enhanced liquidity replaces the incentives to acquire the material information with a belief that a quick exit is possible in the event of disappointment. Chapter 7 explores the supply of credit, generally, and the role of banks, specifically, in creating the timely funding needed to support the upward spiral of speculation and investment under conditions of true uncertainty. It considers, in a manner consistent with Schumpeter and Wicksell, the way in which bank credit creates savings and, in a manner consistent with Minsky, the endogenously fragile nature of this credit. The combined effect is to hazard a greater aggregate ignorance and fragility than that which might exist in the absence of these institutions. The implication is that by creating financial institutions designed to promote efficiency and reduce uncertainty in the capitalist system, we open the door to an instability that can, at times and contrary to the original motivations, reduce efficiency and increase uncertainty.

Speculation via financial equities

In revisiting the nature of speculation under the assumption that financial equities are importantly distinct from the underlying real assets, this exercise illustrates and emphasises the importance to speculation of the *form* in which one holds title to an asset. Contrary to the certain world with complete information wherein financial equities as share claims on a firm's real assets are valued on a *pro rata* basis consistent with the fundamental value of the underlying real assets of the firm, in the real world information is incomplete and the fundamentals are ill defined. As such, the conversion of real asset values into divisible and transferable financial claims valued in money terms is incomplete as well. Analogous in some respects to Georg

Simmel's (1990 [1907]: 404–409) difference in value between personal achievement and some monetary counterpart, the intrinsic value of real assets exceeds its monetary counterpart by an incalculable amount. The loss in value of which is spoken of here arises from an inability to translate completely and perfectly into numerical value such non-quantifiable influences as knowledge, the quality of management, the degree of control over capital and the degree of liquidity.

In the process of 'commodifying' intangible knowledge assets, we actually change and diminish the intrinsic nature of the knowledge itself. To assign monetary values to any object, it is necessary to quantify, in a recognisable way, the characteristics of that object. Where the characteristics of knowledge are inherently qualitative, the best we might do is establish the legal means of identifying and quantifying either the process associated with applying that knowledge (e.g. patents) or the products of having acquired that knowledge (e.g. trademarks and education credentials).[1] Further complicating the exercise of quantifying the value of knowledge is the fact that in the translation process, we may actually distort and diminish the quality of the very object we are attempting to measure. With the attention of assessors increasingly focused on the quantitative measures of knowledge and skill, combined with the predominance of illusions to objective cost–benefits analyses, we are beginning to lose our intuitive appreciation for qualitative values and risk, believing – or acting as though we believe – that the quantitative values are adequate. Where 'credentialized' metrics of knowledge incompletely capture and reflect the true value of knowledge, exclusive focus on monetary values must be perforce inaccurate. Exclusive appeal to objectified measures of costs and benefits removes from 'rational' decision the qualitative value of such elements as educational expertise and managerial quality.

The absence of any personal acquaintance between owners and managers of capital eliminates a critical source of information about management quality. Where personal relationships have the potential to provide information about those qualitative aspects of management so difficult to measure, the impersonal relationship between the 'saving-investor' and the 'saving-receiver' offers no such benefit.[2] Moreover, in the modern industrial firm, there is an additional, ill-definable value contributed by scope economies. Alfred Chandler (1990: 15) defines the modern industrial firm as a

> collection of operating units, each with its own specific facilities and personnel, whose combined resources and activities are co-ordinated, monitored, and allocated by a hierarchy of middle and top managers. It is the existence of this hierarchy that makes the activities and operations of the whole enterprise more than the sum of its operating units.

But how much more and how these additional functions are to be valued is difficult to determine. The *quality* of management – partly captured as the interdependent advantages arising from economies of scope in the production and distribution of products – is a factor that translates impossibly into any objectively defined numerical value.

The absence of information about management quality is compounded by both the loss and relinquishment of control over capital by its owners. The legal partitioning of the value of large-scale enterprises into share claims that are low enough in denomination to be owned by the small saver has gone a great distance to promote effectively the democratisation of wealth and ownership of capital. But the corollary of widespread ownership of capital is diluted interest in its control, a loss of personal acquaintance with the management, and conflicting temporal incentives. 'Security capitalism thus effects democratization of the ownership of capital but brings about monopolization of the control of capital' (Edwards, 1967 [1938]: 5–6).[3] Where more individuals share stakes in an enterprise, each individual commands less of an ability to influence management and thus control capital. Conversely, where capital markets are completely illiquid,

> then there would be no separation of ownership and control. Once some volume of real investment was committed, the owners would have an incentive to use the existing facilities in the best possible way no matter what unforeseen circumstances might arise over the life of plant and equipment.
>
> (Davidson, 1999 [1998]: 283)

The ease with which financial asset ownership can be transferred compounds the loss of control with a relinquishment of what little control remains. Liquidity, as the means to sell an asset quickly at close to current market price, adds yet another source of ill-definable value but shifts the temporal horizon of the owners of capital to a much shorter term. Although the enterprise is a longer-term venture, there are, in a system of financial capitalism, fewer longer-term stakeholders in its success. Shareholders dissatisfied with the operation and direction of the firm are less likely to exert pressure to change and more likely to abandon the enterprise altogether by selling their shares (Schleifer and Vishny, 1986). The telescoping of investor horizons feeds back, placing a greater managerial emphasis on current profits and current capital gains than would otherwise be placed. The result is a greater impatience and shiftability of capital of the type stressed by Keynes (1973a [1936], for example).

Further complicating the exercise of objectively valuing financial equities is the intrusion of opinion. The more that conversion from real to financial values distorts information, the greater the erosion of the influence of purely analytical factors over the market price of financial equities. When combined with conflicting incentive structures and standard credit practices, the door is opened to the influence of other collective and non-analytical factors. As the estimate of future profitability becomes less clear, factors other than discounted future profits may weigh more heavily in the investor's calculation of the related security's price. As Graham and Dodd (1934: 23, original emphases) noted in their influential analysis of securities values:

> ...the influence of what we call analytical factors over the market price is both *partial* and *indirect* – partial, because it frequently competes with purely speculative factors which influence the price in opposite direction; and indirect, because it acts through the intermediary of people's sentiments and decisions. In other words, the market is not a *weighing machine*, on which the value of each issue is recorded by an exact and impersonal mechanism, in accordance with its specific qualities. Rather should we say that the market is a *voting machine*, whereon countless individuals register choices which are the product partly of reason and partly of emotion.

As with all voting opportunities, a crowd-mind may develop independently of the objective facts of the situation. Where opinion can influence the outcome, no numerical value can be assigned to the probability of that outcome – a point colourfully illustrated by Keynes in his account of the court debates around the appropriate damages to be awarded a woman who had not been given reasonable opportunity to win a British beauty contest (see Chapter 4, n.1).

A deterioration of information quality, a loss of information, the telescoping of investor horizons and an intrusion of opinion create a potential instability in financial equities where none would exist in the underlying real assets. Consequently, we might register qualified disagreement with Charles Kindleberger's (1989: 20) claim that 'the object of speculation may vary widely from one mania or bubble to the next'. By identifying a long list of real assets as the objects of historical speculation, Kindleberger suggests that individually canals, selected companies – new, existing and merged – are all equally susceptible to speculation. However, many of the episodes identified by Kindleberger entailed speculation via marketable financial instruments. By classifying speculative objects based on the *form* in which one holds title to the asset, we reduce significantly the list of speculative objects and move a little closer to a clearer, institutionally grounded understanding of financial instability. Were we to stop here, however, we would have only partially clarified Kindleberger's assessment of potential speculations and environments.

Revolutionary innovation and speculation

Historically, many dramatic episodes of Western financial crises have been preceded by intense speculation in financial assets associated with revolutionary innovations. In addition to the crises which occurred in the process of adopting such revolutionary technologies as the steam engine (Britain, US and Continental Europe 1847/48, 1857, and US 1873), the internal combustion engine, electronic and chemical innovations (US 1929), there are those that occurred in the wake of revolutionary innovations in institutional structures. The introduction of the joint-stock company, for example, was a critical component of both the 1720 'South Sea Bubble' and the 1721 French 'Mississippi Bubble'.[4]

In the period preceding these and other crises, there is evidence of spreading enthusiasm for revolutionary developments – developments that must have been little understood by virtue of the novelty. Such an environment of uncertain promise suggests an optimistic ignorance on the part of speculators. This ignorance is both partial and of a particular kind. A given revolutionary innovation has, in its early stages of being transformed from invention to innovation, great potential. But the uniqueness of the nascent innovation prevents any inference about any probability of success. Without repeated trials from which to measure probabilities, we have Frank Knight's (1964 [1921]: 225–226) 'estimates' for which 'there is *no valid basis of any kind* for classifying instances'. It is George Shackle's (1949) 'crucial' experiment. In such situations it is 'manifestly meaningless' to speak of the probability of any degree of error in this judgement.

The exercise of 'knowing' is complicated further by the fact that for innovations to be revolutionary they must eventually assert some degree of universal impact. Such impact is in no small way the product of widening opinion as to the usefulness or desirability of the innovation. As Nathan Rosenberg (1994: 3) reminds us, however, 'it appears that it has been remarkably difficult to appreciate the potential significance of an invention at the time of its first introduction'.

Research into the history and economics of technology highlights the uncertainty inherent in the gradual adaptation and adoption of a given invention. '(Historical) analysis supports the view that technological change often takes place in quite information-poor and uncertain environments' (Rosenberg, 1994: 5). Stress is laid on the clustering of complementary inventions and on the advances necessary to yield the ultimate economic, technological and societal impact. Emphasis is placed, too, on both the costs of developing the new technology and the variety of costs associated with replacing older infrastructures – physical as well as cultural and educational.[5]

Subsequent to the initial creation and development of the innovation, the diffusion of the innovation is gradual and its success is conditional on gaining wider recognition and appreciation of its potential. As most revolutionary changes have come from outside of the authority structures of established industries, the process of diffusion and gradual acceptance has been at times slow. Rosenberg (1994) presents clear evidence and argument supporting the notion that from initial invention to widespread adoption of an innovation, the path is long, evolutionary (in the sense of exhibiting path dependence), and non-linear in many respects.

> Thus, the speed with which inventions are transformed into innovations, and consequently diffused, will depend upon the actual *and* expected trajectory of performance improvement and cost reduction.... [T]here may be a highly non-linear relationship between rates of improvement in a new product and rates of adoption. Further there is often a long gestation period in the development of a new technology during which gradual improvements are not exploited because costs of the new technology are still substantially in excess of the old. However, as the threshold level is approached and pierced, adoption rates of the new technology become increasingly sensitive to further improvements.
>
> (Rosenberg, 1994: 69)

Initially, only those intimately associated with the inventions have had the possibility of imagining any of the potential. In the early stages of advance, it is in no way reasonable to expect that predictions of future profitability would be or could be possible, at least not reliably so. If a calculus of probabilities is impossible, the question of the motive to speculate arises. More than a 'spontaneous urge to action', it is the opportunity to partake in the ill-defined *chance* of an innovation's success. Individuals vary in their willingness to take such chances with their investment, and Chandler (1990) differentiates conceptually between those individuals who invest first in an uncertain but hopeful enterprise and those who follow once the first trials prove positive. The 'first mover' is that individual who is aware of the invention and acts on intuition, a 'hunch', that the invention may yield potential benefits. Initial success appears in the technology itself as an interdependent combination of gradual technological improvements and diffusion.

With no ability to forecast future profitability in the early stages of diffusion, there is no way to estimate expected downside losses of any investment in a revolutionary innovation. Losses are perceived, nevertheless, to be limited for the individual where financial commitments made are small and liquid. Share ownership allows the individual speculator a choice over the magnitude of her or his commitment and lessens significantly the perceived threat of substantial loss. Rosenberg and Birdzell (1986) and Rosenberg (1994) argue that it is precisely the institutional devices of limited liability, tradable and marketable share ownership that is central from the point of view of facilitating investment in risky undertakings. Levine and Zervos (1998) demonstrate that in recent years for a broad range of countries, stock market liquidity and size (among other variables) are robustly correlated with productivity improvements (see also King and Levine, 1993). Keynes argues that investors may be nonetheless willing to speculate in an uncertain outcome if the commitment made is liquid. 'For the fact that each individual investor flatters himself that his commitment is "liquid" (though this cannot be true for all investors collectively) calms his nerves and makes him much more willing to run a risk' (Keynes, 1973a [1936]: 160).[6]

When offered the opportunity to speculate in liquid claims on an innovation, the absence of information is of less concern. In the early stages of diffusion, professional speculators – who are otherwise best adept at processing information and deciding courses of action – are now confronted with a situation in which information is deficient and cannot be processed reliably through the existing internal models and outcomes cannot be calculated. A growing optimism about the ill-defined potential of assets related to an innovation forces professional speculators to rely more on current information – opinion and recent price movements – and to exhibit increasingly predictable patterns of rule-governed behaviour. When speculators extrapolate from recent price movements to anticipate future yields, it is the simple rule of 'positive feedback trading' – buying because prices have been rising – that governs their behaviour.

Initial success stimulates professional speculative activity in at least three ways. First, is the suggestion that in default of any ability to forecast future fundamentals in periods of extreme uncertainty, professional speculators will extrapolate from a recent price increase. This 'naïve' dependence on available information about recent price changes is a dependence created in default of any other means by which to predict future prospects. It is a dynamic extension of Keynes's static analysis of individual behaviour and judgement in the face of true uncertainty as described earlier. Recent price increases – the continuation of which others affirm – forms the primary basis upon which individual speculators – professional and naïve alike – anticipate future price increases. De Long *et al.* (1990) demonstrate that when some market participants follow positive feedback trading strategies, it may be optimal for others to 'jump on the bandwagon' themselves. Second, industry pressures may contribute further stimulation. David

Scharfstein and Jeremy Stein (1990) demonstrate the important influence of relative portfolio returns and professional reputation in encouraging the herd behaviour of portfolio managers.[7] Third, to the extent professionals recognise the potential self-fulfilling nature of widespread expectations of speculative asset price increases, they may include their judgement of market 'mood' as independent information.

As with the first movers responsible for bringing the revolutionary invention to market, professional speculators are the ones to undertake the first trials in the affiliated financial speculation. The simplified and easily predicted behaviour of the professional speculator has the effect of rendering markets more comprehensible to the amateur at a time when attentions are increasingly focused on the widening impact of the innovation. An increasing number of people affected by the innovation seek to comprehend the unusual and unusually optimistic situation. Once the empowering symbol of financial speculation emerges in an acquisitive culture, so too does the leadership of the professional speculator. Thus, at a time when an increasing number of people eagerly seek some interpretation of the changes, the potential followers more easily understand the message communicated by the leaders.

Communication networks are essential for broadcasting the success of others and feeding the attendant enthusiasm. Networks for the distribution of information include the formal networks established by the media and the informal networks inherent in personal kinship and community ties. In contemporary society, Ralph Turner and Lewis Killian (1987) suggest that the media operate as something more than vehicles for the neutral transmission of facts; they operate as a change agent and as a means of moulding public opinion. Larry Samuelson (2004) argues that public information may serve as a 'coordinating device' that gives rise to self-fulfilling expectations,[8] and Robert Shiller (2002: 71) points out that the 'history of speculative bubbles begins roughly with the advent of the newspaper'.[9] The extent to which the media can and do successfully contribute to a rising enthusiasm by selecting and highlighting the astounding successes of a few is beyond doubt.

Increased public attention on the speculation, which is afforded and promoted by communication networks in a culture that values material wealth, encourages more individuals to participate when recent past success – as simply indicated in the rising price of the speculative asset – legitimates the extrapolated expectations. Rising asset prices reinforce the belief in the appropriateness of the speculation, reassuring professionals and amateurs alike. As Turner and Killian (1987: 9) elaborate: 'While people act on impressions, their impressions are constantly tested in action. The . . . success of initial actions may produce . . . the increased assurance that fosters more courageous action.'

The initial successes of both real and financial investments alike encourage others to contemplate imitation. Naïve speculators jump into the market in significant and increasing numbers once speculation in financial equities related to the innovation becomes a keynoted activity. The increased public attention received by reported capital gains captures the attention of prior non-participants who mentally calculate how much they would have made had they bought when they first considered such action. The success of an increasing number of persons with whom the prospective speculator has some connection feeds the impression of feasibility and further encourages the taking of action. Ultimately, getting rich quickly attracts new speculators, the fear of being left behind repels them from sitting any longer on the sidelines, and the recent success of others makes them much less cautious.

Fashionable imitation is an essential ingredient to both the diffusion of an innovation and the spreading of a speculative enthusiasm. The opportunity to imitate the professional speculators requires the institutional accessibility of equity markets to the small saver.[10] Historically, there have been critical developments in the evolution of financial capitalism that have been pivotal in rendering financial equity markets significantly more accessible at a time when the society was undergoing changes introduced by other, non-financial, revolutionary innovations. The introduction of the joint-stock company in both England and France in the late 1600s and early 1700s revolutionised social relations. For the first time, wealth was obtainable by a means other than birthright. Significantly restricted by legislation shortly after the South Sea Bubble collapsed, England saw the reintroduction of the unspecified institution of joint-stock ownership a century later. Examples that are more recent include the introduction of the discount broker in the 1980s, and the Internet access afforded by the evolving innovations in information and communications technologies in the 1990s. In each case, the market was rendered considerably more accessible to the small saver-investor at a time when a revolutionary innovation was dramatically altering the social and economic landscape. In each instance, these compounding developments contributed significantly to the contemporaneous episodes of an intense speculative enthusiasm by enhancing the ease with which the non-professional imitator–speculator could participate.

Consideration of the institutional characteristics of the market for financial equities reveals an erosion of the quality and quantity of information, the presence of non-quantifiable influences, and the possibility of an unconstrained credit-financed pyramiding of asset prices. This brief exercise restates insights articulated by early writers of finance capitalism in a way that permits an appreciation of the importance of these institutional devices in the current context. Following George Edwards (1967

[1938]) and others, the conversion from real to financial equity introduces an independent source of uncertainty. The conversion of real assets into their financial equity counterpart entails a loss of information about critical non-quantifiable influences such as entrepreneurial quality, scope economies and networks critical to the diffusion of an innovation. The conversion of illiquid physical assets into more liquid marketable shares of an enterprise explains the persistence of the information deficiency in the sense that it rationalises the ignorance. Where the acquired asset is liquid, at least in normal times, it is individually cost-efficient to ignore the lost information. The introduction of liquid marketable shares encourages at once greater savings and a greater fickleness or impatience on the part of the investor. Intrusion of speculator opinion and other collective influences occur in response to the uncertainty, creating further uncertainty for all speculators. For these reasons, objective calculations of future returns to financial assets are difficult to calculate in normal times. In extraordinary times, such as those defined by the adaptation to a revolutionary innovation, all attempts to forecast on the basis of fundamental information perforce must be abandoned and replaced with simple rule governed behaviour based on extrapolations from recent experience.

The development of a mania is the gradual spreading of a speculative euphoria – one that becomes increasingly intense. It is the gradual swell of enthusiasm marked by an increasing participation of new and naïve speculators who are motivated more by collective actions and less by any independent objective decision to participate. The corresponding geometric rate at which the speculative activity and excitement spreads manifests itself in a spiralling upward of asset prices that parallels the non-linear diffusion path of the precipitating innovation. This reasoning suggests that episodes of extreme financial instability in the liquid claims on some assets are the exaggerated mirror image of the non-linear, evolutionary path marking the diffusion of a revolutionary innovation. The suggested pattern of instability in asset prices is similar to that of the traditional story summarised in Chapter 5, but the explanation for this instability is now perhaps more understandable. Indeed, beyond investigating how individuals reasonably behave in the face of a growing optimistic uncertainty that parallels the diffusion of the innovation, there is little else that changes. All observable results go through as before. Initial speculation gathers momentum as the first results prove positive, credit to finance both primary and secondary speculation is extended, and a self-perpetuating rise in the market prices of related assets appears.

In this way, the norm of financial speculation emerges; but it cannot continue forever. Geometrically rising asset prices will eventually raise questions about the future profits and discount rates required to support contemporaneous price levels. Whatever doubts appear and for however long they persist, at some point these questions will be answered. Until we reach this point, however, assessing the reasonableness of the speculation or the height of asset prices throughout the diffusion process is problematic. What constitutes *excess* speculation throughout the diffusion of an innovation is wholly unclear. There are no criteria that permit, *ex ante*, estimation of an asset's fundamental value. Hence, we are incapable of estimating any benchmark from which to measure deviations along the path of diffusion of an innovation. All that exists as potentially observable measures of instability or fragility are those movements and actions that are characteristic of an optimistically uncertain environment. On the equities side, this appears simply as an increasing predominance of 'positive feedback trading' – buying that is motivated by anticipated gains which are justified only by past price increases.

7 The other side of the coin

The influence of credit creation and banks on speculation

Equities will, as we have seen, go some distance to encourage and facilitate the process of investment and innovation. Introducing the complementary possibility of borrowing to fund speculation in an innovation's assets can contribute further to the self-perpetuating speculative advance. Borrowing to finance purchases of financial claims on these assets compounds the possibilities all the more. This chapter explores the endogenous credit dynamics that support and promote speculation in periods of optimistic uncertainty. It considers endogenous credit demand generated by stock pyramiding and endogenous debt structures of the type discussed by Hyman Minsky (1986, 1982a). In situations where optimistic uncertainty dominates and financial institutions offer elastically supplied credit, there exists the potential for demand-driven credit expansions (of the type discussed by Moore, 1988) to support the speculation. When we allow for the possibility that banks are more than simply agents brokering the exchange of loanable funds – when the operation of banks must be viewed as the institutional creators of credit – we are a step closer to understanding the importance of finance in creating the intrinsic instability of the finance capitalist system. As Joseph Schumpeter (1994 [1954]: 1114) notes in his assessment of the role banks play:

> The theory of 'credit creation' not only recognizes patent facts without obscuring them by artificial constructions; it also brings the peculiar mechanism of saving and investment that is characteristic of fullfledged capitalist society and the true role of banks in capitalist evolution.

Credit

Easy credit terms and frequent reassessments of market value generate additional value which stimulates and motivates the speculation. With no means other than high and rising prices to verify the value of the collateral security, creditors are constrained in their ability to assess appropriate credit limits. That creditors might also be subject to fashionable professional pressures – pressures that encourage herding in precisely the same way as that which influences professional speculators – further feeds the excitement.

There is substantial evidence that credit expansion could be the result, rather than the cause, of a speculative boom. From at least John Stuart Mill (1967 [1826]) to more recent technical studies such as that by Barry Eichengreen and Kris Mitchener (2003), an abundance of argument and empirical evidence suggest that accommodating credit expansion contributes to an economic expansion.[1] Should the cost of available credit be low relative to the anticipated returns, then access to brokers' loans for purchasing stocks on margin can aggravate stock price changes in both rising and falling markets.[2] In a rising market, investor claims on capital gains furnish the basis on which to acquire additional credit that is used to buy additional shares and that can drive up prices further (see Bogen and Krooss, 1960, as cited in Fortune, 2001). In a manner reminiscent of Knut Wicksell's pure credit economy, so long as the net sellers of shares deposit the proceeds in the market or institution responsible for extending margin credit, there is nothing institutionally that will impose an upper limit to this credit-pyramiding effect (see Luckett, 1982). The reverse holds true in a falling market, where price decreases erase equity, force margin calls and force sales of stocks, which further depresses prices in a manner akin to Fisher's debt-deflation process. Such an endogenous credit expansion/contraction process is apparent in Mill's account of the British nineteenth century British episodes, in Carl Snyder's (1930) explanation of the over 180 per cent increase in call loan volume between 1927 and 1929 in the United States (see also Eiteman, 1933), and is consistent with Peter Fortune's (2001) analysis of the most recent American experience. Moreover, Fortune finds that while a high level of margin loans indicates upward pressure in rising markets and vice versa in falling markets, this effect was greater in the more speculative NASDAQ market leading up to its peak in the year 2000 than it was in the market for mature issues (S&P 500) for the same period.

Hyman Minsky (1982a,b, 1986) views the mania–crisis experience as one which differs from all credit-induced business fluctuations in magnitude alone. The further we move away from the last downturn, the greater the fragility of the markets and, hence, the more severe will be the next episode. Minsky's credit cycle concentrates on the nature of the debt incurred to finance enterprise and its relation to the investment's income stream. As an economic upswing progresses, Minsky's investors, all of whom must rely on current and recent historical information alone, become 'heartened by the success of the boom', and increase their tendency to accept larger doses of debt to finance investment. An endogenous element to the process is introduced by identifying three sources of funds from which to service this debt: current income, revenue from the sale of assets, and the issue of new debt. As the memory of the last distress recedes, increased leverage is encouraged by the fact that, throughout the course of the boom, short-term interest rates lie below long-term rates. Those in need of longer term funds are, thus, tempted into the shorter term debt market. The increasing demand for short-term loanable funds drives up the cost of those funds and, in the face of a growing mismatch of maturities, increases the fragility of the financial markets. The margin of a firm's fiscal safety (the difference between the present value of assets and the price of investment output) decreases as the proportion of debt service rises from rising interest rates. Over time, rising debt charges exceed current income, forcing debtors to finance their debt by either revenue from the sale of assets or by the issue of new debt.

Minsky's Financial Instability Hypothesis focuses attention on streams of asset income (rather than on the fundamentals defined as the discounted value of these streams) in excess of contemporaneous changes in debt service costs. Fluctuations in these margins of safety explain the time path of asset prices; financing incentives induce short-term borrowing to finance long-term expenditures and financing constraints drive up debt service costs. As the rising debt service costs outpace increases in income, borrowers must rely more on capital gains (and less on sustainable income generated by the asset itself) to service debt – markedly increasing fragility. Competitive pressures ensures borrowing continues in the face of rising debt costs, with rising equity prices appearing to validate the new debt assumed. In this way, debtors increasingly and unintentionally shift to this tenuous form of 'Ponzi' financing. Money, created in the process of financing positions in assets increases whenever bankers share in a speculative optimism that supports and reaffirms the belief that borrowers positions in assets will generate sufficient cash flows (see Papadimitriou and Wray, 2001; I will return to this point below). Reminiscent of Walter Bagehot (1873), a limited memory of the maturity risk allows the activity to continue until such time as debt service costs swamp returns from all sources and bankruptcy is forced.

In a fashion parallel to the manner in which a protracted speculation in assets generates endogenously a narrowing of the corridor of stability, the margins of debtor safety begin to fall over time.[3] 'Consequently, the width of the corridor of stability could narrow during a long boom, in keeping with Minsky's discussions of the changing stability of the economy as financial structure changes over the course of the cycle (Minsky 1982a, 1986). This was Irving Fisher's explanation of why the sharp deflation of

1920–1921 did not result in a great depression: inside debt denominated in fixed nominal terms, was significantly smaller relative to the size of the economy in 1920–1921 than in 1929 (Fisher, 1932, 1933)' (Dimand, 2005: 194). This notion of a corridor of stability is akin to Leijonhufvud's (1981 [1973]: 129) notion adapted to permit an endogenous determination of the thresholds.

What constitutes *excess* debt in this framework is now, however, problematic. Without an ability to estimate future profitability, we lack the means to assess the appropriateness of the level of debt incurred. Of course, *after* a collapse, speculation was unwarranted and the debt assumed to support it too great. In the midst of a speculation, however, it is impossible to identify uniquely and precisely that level of prices that is 'excessive' and thus that level of debt that is 'unwarranted'. Eichengreen and Mitchener (2003: 32), for example, attempt, with some effort, to differentiate a credit boom from one that relies on the interpretation of a stock price bubble as an explanation of the 1920s experience. The point of this study is that speculation under uncertainty renders the traditional concept of a bubble irrelevant and that it is precisely the speculation on an optimistically uncertain future that calls forth the credit to support it. As such, the speculation and the credit expansion are, contrary to motivation of the earlier mentioned study, if the reader will forgive the pun, simply two sides of the 'same coin'.

Banks and bank credit

When the transaction entails costs of searching and locating potential savers and borrowers, assessing creditworthiness of the borrowers and negotiating the terms of the contracts, the introduction of an intermediary with a specialisation in the administration, monitoring, and execution of such exchanges will reduce these costs. When the specialist intermediary simply brokers the exchange – such as happens in the markets for debt – there is no material difference in the economic outcome beyond that which can be measured by the diminution of transactions costs.

The public's relative unfamiliarity with the debt (and equity) markets, the markets' inaccessibility to small savers, and the high costs of assessing creditworthiness of small, prospective borrowers, preclude participation in financial markets for many (though, at times of heightened optimism, more are tempted into the equity markets). The introduction of the specialist intermediary as a party to the exchange of funds between two ultimate principals – where here the intermediary is at once a borrower from the saver and a lender to the user of funds – further promotes the accumulation and allocation of savings by rendering the credit arrangement more widely accessible. With specialists intermediating financial transactions by signing contracts with lenders separately from those they sign with borrowers, specialists have the opportunity to alter the terms and conditions of the contract as funds pass between them. For example, the intermediary may collect from several small savers in low denominations, and lend the combined amount to one borrower seeking to finance a larger project.

If this specialist intermediary is constructed as a 'deposit bank' – issuing highly liquid, transferable, deposit balances – as substitutes for currency – in exchange for debt contracts, we introduce the potential of radically altering the influence credit has on both the economy and the society. The portfolios of deposit banks are unique in at least a couple of respects. Unlike any other intermediary, the bank acquires longer term, income-earning assets by issuing shorter term liabilities (deposit balances) against itself. Moreover, these liabilities are convertible on demand at par into cash. Historically, the assets acquired are predominantly business loans and loans to the government. So long as business confidence remains stable, bank-issued credit, and its offsetting deposit liabilities, ensure and support the successful day-to-day operation of economic activity. When confidence changes – rising with the spread of speculative optimism and falling with the spread of pessimism – credit expands or contracts in step, and in periods of extreme pessimism, preference for holding cash can overtake the public's willingness to hold bank money. If the rate at which confidence changes is gradual enough to allow the bank time to properly adjust its portfolio of assets, there need be no drastic consequences. If, however, the change in confidence is sudden and extreme – as is the case when panic sets in – the bank's ability to accommodate the sudden increase in the demand for liquidity is severely constrained by its inability to liquidate its longer term assets. When there exists no alternative for meeting the increased demand for cash (or at the point that it is exhausted), bank runs of the type analysed by Douglas Diamond and Philip Dybvig (1983) will threaten solvency. By the mere fact that confidence is socially constructed and contagious, the level of credit as measured by the size of the bank's loan portfolio, together with the degree of liquidity, has the potential to become more than a bell-weather of business confidence but a fundamental factor that influences that confidence.

While banks rarely finance revolutionary technological innovations at the outset, they have backed the credit supporting margin purchases of shares in revolutionary developments (such as in England in 1720 and in the United States in the 1920s), they have been the ultimate source of credit by means of discounting bills of exchange (such as in England 1825 and 1847), and they have extended credit to develop infrastructure related to a revolutionary reorganisation of the economy (such as in Thailand in the 1990s). As well, banks commonly finance the adoption of innovation by imitators, thus promoting the spread and diffusion of the innovation. As Rondo Cameron and Hugh Patrick (1967: 13) put it,

> Under normal circumstances bankers will prefer to lend to profitable, growing firms and industries rather than to stagnant and declining ones. Thus, while it is rare for banks to finance directly a period of experimentation with a completely novel production technique by a new, inexperienced businessman or inventor…it is quite common for bankers to finance the expansion of firms that have already introduced successful innovations, and a lot to finance the adoption of the innovation by imitators.

The outstanding innovation in finance in the nineteenth century was the substitution of various forms of bank-created money for commodity money. With the growth in the 1820s of non-note-issuing joint-stock banks, bank deposits came to 'occupy an important place in the stock of money or current means of payment in England'. As a result, the use of bank money as a substitute for commodity money 'gave to bankers, the specialists and presumed experts in the business of lending to deficit units, a large leverage over real resources which they could transfer directly to enterprising entrepreneurs' (Cameron, 1967b: 315–316).

In this substitution, the possibility of endogenous credit creation is introduced in a manner consistent with the 'Banking School' view maintained by Thomas Tooke, John Fullarton, and others (see Mints, 1945). It was later developed by Nicholas Kaldor (1982) and Basil Moore (1988) and formed an essential component of Minsky's hypothesis. In this view, causation runs from prices to credit, rather than in the opposite direction as proponents of modern-day inflation-stability policies maintain. To use Axel Leijonhufvud's (1998: 211) characterisation, speculative booms of the type that precede a crisis are 'inside' money inflations 'fuelled by cumulative expansions of bank (and other forms of) credit. In these the ratio [of inside to outside money] rises. These inside money inflations cannot be sustained indefinitely, therefore, without ending in a financial crash'.[4]

When credit is elastically supplied by deposit banks, then a number of factors can influence the amount of credit at any given time through alterations in both the total volume and the velocity of circulation of different types of exchange instruments rendering the threshold ratio of inside to outside money variable and unpredictable. Optimism (or pessimism) importantly influences banks' willingness to extend credit limits in the manner suggested by Minsky. As well, financial innovation can alter the relative velocities of newer versus older media of exchange. The introduction of innovative financial instruments or processes changes the relative velocities of circulation in ways that cannot be measured at the time the innovation occurs. The effective 'quantity' of the total exchange media for the purpose of supporting transactions, becomes impossible to measure contemporaneously with any accuracy.

The importance of banks stretches, then, beyond the simple extension of borrowing and lending opportunities to persons otherwise unlikely or unable to access debt or equity markets. Where bank-issued liabilities (deposit balances) dominate a nation's media of exchange and short-term bank loans provide the major source of working capital, a successful banking system aids importantly the operation of daily business transactions that define the nation's economy. These additional functions alone confer on banks a unique importance in the economy. Now banks are more than simply efficient, complementary, alternatives to the transfer of funds from savers to borrowers – they become an intrinsic part of the credit creation process that can increase the opportunities to innovate and accumulate beyond which would otherwise be the case. In other words, 'maximum output' and 'capacity' are not immutable physical limits but instead, limits that are endogenous to the operation of the banking system and extension of credit.

The worst financial crises in history have involved the collapse of the banking system. By its economic importance alone, this historical observation is, perhaps, now well understood. The importance of banks extends, however, beyond the economic into the social. At the level of the individual transaction, bankers familiar with their customers, have access to qualitative information on both the customer and the customer's enterprise for which the customer employs the borrowed funds – information that allows for a fuller assessment of default risk and may actually contribute to a reduction of it. Bankers, with whom borrowers have a relationship, become partners in the borrower's enterprise.

Bankers share a stake in the success of the commercial business, possibly by holding a lien on collateral assets or simply in their concern for bank solvency. The borrower, conversely, has a personal stake in avoiding bankruptcy – where now, the costs of default include a cost to the borrower's reputation and relationship with the banker. As individuals operating in a capitalist system, however, bankers are not immune to the pressures imposed by a culture of capitalism and with it, the waves of optimism and pessimism that can emerge. Given bankers' willingness and ability to create and destroy credit as confidence flows and ebbs, bankers are in a unique position to contribute significantly to the evolution of a speculative enthusiasm or its recoil in crisis.

At the level of the social, banks are conservative institutions with a reputation for and a history of safety and soundness. Unlike financial markets in many ways, banks are, in a Durkheimian sense, institutions that contribute to the stability of the social order. Banks offer a safe haven for the savings of those who work hard and save against unforeseen contingencies. They offer a means of managing liquidity to smooth consumption and production over time for the many households and business too small, too unfamiliar with, too risk averse, and too otherwise preoccupied to participate in the markets. They offer an accessible and familiar opportunity to accumulate wealth. And when they collapse, not only does the event threaten the whole payments system of a nation and risk the elimination of small savings, but the collapse rends the very fabric of the social system of which the banks are a significant part.

In sum, the economic importance of a financial exchange between those with surplus funds and those in need of funds is, in the first instance, the opportunity to render savings productive. The introduction of equities, credit (debt) markets and banks, reduce transactions costs and thus promote the transfer of funds from savers to borrowers, rendering savings 'productive'. But more than simply the opportunity to channel savings into investment to ensure maximum output and productive capacity, the introduction of these institutions alters economic potential. Economic output, the corresponding level of employment, and its distribution over different industries, are now dependent on the extent to and manner in which credit institutions, generally, and banks, particularly, operate within the society. To the extent that credit is dependent on the level of confidence in future economic prospects, any change to that confidence alters the extension and distribution of credit. When waves of optimism can call forth credit to support the activity that focuses that mood, credit operates to ensure the optimism becomes self-fulfilling in every real economic sense. When credit is acquired by issuing highly liquid transferable claims against a bank, these claims become an integral part of the payments system, augmenting the circulating media of exchange. Where banks are also conservative pillars of society, these institutions serve as a stabilising social force. For the very reason banks play such critical economic and social roles, bank failures will have uniquely, devastating effects.

From the previous chapters, the conditions under which speculative optimism appear may now be clear enough. The questions that remain are what cause a shift away from that optimism; what sparks a panic in a distressed environment? To these questions I now turn.

8 Recoil in crisis

From peak to panic

It is a commonly held belief that a financial crisis and panic mark the end of a speculative mania, with the extent and intensity of the alarm mirroring the extent and intensity of the preceding enthusiasm. While panics have never appeared independently of a prior mania, a crisis-crowd dynamic has not always developed in the wake of an intense euphoric speculation and never has it occurred the very moment the mania subsided. In the highest profile episodes, the panic appeared weeks, sometimes months, after the enthusiasm dissipated. In one of the earliest episodes in England, shares in the South Sea Company reached their peak in August of 1720. Over the next month share prices declined steadily to half their value. It was on the 17th of September 1720 that panic erupted. Share prices dropped to one-third of the price they commanded eleven days earlier. A similar time lag between the peak of share prices and the eruption of a panic marks the end of several other high profile speculations in Western financial history.

This chapter explores the cause of financial distress experienced in the wake of a recession of speculative enthusiasm and considers the conditions under which that distress could erupt into a panic. In the view expressed here, speculation subsides, in a Schumpeterian manner, when the impulse to innovate recedes. Depending on the extent of the revealed deviation of market prices from exposed fundamentals as well as the relative debt burdens, the end of the speculation may or may not be followed by a reversal of fortune. The preconditions of distress derive, then, from the debt incurred to finance a speculation in the optimistic promise of an innovation of uncertain potential. The potential for a panic derives from the threats posed by a sudden deterioration in liquidity in a distressed environment.

Peak and distress

The onset of crisis has variously been identified as a 'sudden collapse' of financial market prices (including currency values), illiquidity causing a suspension of convertibility at some previously fixed rate (either internally in the case of banks suspending convertibility of deposits into domestic currency or externally in the case of a nation suspending convertibility of its currency into alternative currencies or specie) and the exhaustion of either bank capital or international reserves.[1] These crises may relate to or evolve into a debt crisis wherein debtors of some significance are unable to service their debts. Where financial crises occur in the wake of an intense speculation, the question is what then causes the reversal of fortune? As part of an evolutionary process that is characterised by the ebb and flow of business activity, the question is essentially one relating to the peak of a business cycle. The economic process envisaged here is one in which the advance and subsequent slowdown are the symptoms of disequilibrium adjustments to fundamental change that has been introduced by an innovation of some consequence. It is one in which the empirical business cycle is driven fundamentally by the ebb and flow of an impulse to innovate, with credit elements compounding and exaggerating the cyclical fluctuations in prices and output.

The complexity of the underlying socio-economic process reveals itself clearly in the attempt to identify those causes that bring the speculation to an end. In purely economic terms, speculation in the assets associated with an innovation via the purchase of equity shares financed by debt entails seven important material elements. There is the physical investment in the assets of the innovation, the future income these assets can reasonably be expected to generate (when capable of being estimated) and the market price of the physical assets themselves. If speculation proceeds through the trading of equity claims on the physical assets, there is, separately, the market price of the share claims. Finally, with debt accumulated to support the speculation, there is the nominal or money value of the debt, the real value of the debt as the money value of the debt in relation to the market value of the underlying asset which the debt financed, and, finally, the cost of the debt itself. If portfolio considerations, with its attendant cost–benefit analysis, guide asset allocation, we can expect to see all these elements assessed in relation to one another. The end of a speculation, if driven solely by economic considerations, would occur when the costs of further speculation outweigh any additional anticipated gains.

The break in the upward momentum occurs when the process reaches a threshold beyond which it cannot continue to replicate itself. The threshold may derive from the cost of debt rising faster than the speculative capital gains, which eventually eliminates the opportunity of any further material gain. Alternatively, the threshold may derive from the limits of investment in the innovation, where profitability eventually revealed cannot support contemporaneous prices in the speculative assets.[2] Further, an emphasis on one does not preclude the importance of the other; the emphasis placed on the relative costs of debt by predominantly monetary theories of the business cycle does not preclude the importance of Schumpeter's notion that underlying innovation fundamentals can too play a causal role.[3] Yet the threshold may not derive from pure economic considerations in the first instance. Mill (1967 [1826]), in his analysis of the 1825–1826 crisis in England, grapples with this question but cannot resolve it satisfactorily. As Evelyn Forget (1990: 634) suggests, we are 'left with the uncomfortable feeling that, for Mill, the mood shifts simply because it shifts'. If the social is to be considered, the norm of a speculation renders out-dated the fashionable elements of the *activity* of speculation, and as an increasing amount of speculative proceeds are converted into luxury goods, the social value of all related fashionable displays of superior status is diminished.

These and other related explanations of the end of a given episode of speculation remain debated. The absence of either historical or theoretical dominance of any one explanation underscores our inability to pinpoint in advance just when a speculative enthusiasm will subside. But subside it will and eventually, perhaps causally, perhaps not, the uncertainty with respect to the future income potential of the speculative assets will be replaced as the full scope of that potential becomes apparent. As suggested by Schumpeter (1939) and elaborately examined by Rosenberg (1994), the innovation eventually reaches its potential and the profitability net of borrowing costs is gradually revealed. With maturation of the innovation and the emergence of current income, it becomes increasingly easier for professional speculators to forecast future income based on forward estimates of performance. Professional speculators gradually replace their extrapolated estimates of future capital gains with some revised internal forecasting model that incorporates this new information. The combination of the emerging fundamentals and the concomitant revision to internal methods of forecasting introduces new ways of assessing the appropriateness of prevailing asset prices. When the newly emerging assessment metrics do not support an expectation of further price increases, professional speculation subsides. When the metrics support a lower market value for the assets, professional speculators may actually reverse their bets, as they did in early 1997 when speculators began trading against the Thai currency. The slowdown in speculative demand for assets, assuming no sharp curtailment of supply, will translate into a slowdown, levelling off or fall in the market prices of these assets.

Depending on the nature and extent of the underlying debt accumulated to finance the speculation, the slowdown alone could be sufficient to create distress and a downward spiral of debt, creating further distress. Should limits on credit growth force up the cost of debt through the earlier speculative stages, Minsky's Ponzi financing situation – wherein speculators are servicing their debt from anticipated capital gains alone – would be endogenous to both the psychology and the economics of the speculative process. Speculators in the midst of the speculative enthusiasm, extrapolating future price increases on the basis of past price increases alone, can only be expecting to service their debt out of future capital gains. If they have been borrowing at increasingly higher rates, then the possibility diminishes over time that any revealed profitability to the speculative asset exceeds the cost of debt. At the point where the cost of debt exceeds the revealed or yet-to-be revealed profitability, the speculators are, in economic terms, Ponzi financers.

The levelling off of asset prices is alone sufficient to cause distress to those indebted speculators who incurred debt anticipating capital gains from which to service or discharge their speculative debt. Any inferior situation in which emerging information suggests that current prices are unjustifiably high will result in a reversal of speculation causing asset prices to fall and an even greater distress to occur. Any price levels deemed unsustainable based on newly revealed fundamentals will decline, however, further distressing all indebted speculators. In the reverse unfolding of events, a fall in the market price of shares eliminates margin collateral. The investor responding to a margin call has the choice of placing additional funds in his or her margin account or selling the shares and discharging the debt. The financial liabilities incurred by a margin investor are, however, unresponsive to market price, being fixed as they are in nominal terms. And it is this long-standing practice of using current market prices to value collateral financial assets but holding liabilities fixed in nominal terms that explains Irving Fisher's paradox. The decline in prices may force a distress sale of collateral assets that, in turn, depresses asset prices. By forcing sales when asset prices are low or falling – sales that drive asset prices down further in an institutional framework that holds the nominal value of debt constant – we obtain the paradoxical result that 'the more debtors pay, the more they owe'. A debt-deflation spiral of this type, as discussed by Fisher (1933), distresses both lenders – who do not recoup total amounts owed through sales of low-valued collateral assets – and other asset holders whose real value of outstanding debt rises.

The collapse of asset prices has the potential to create financing problems for the wider economy through either or both of its primary financing institutions – the capital market and the credit enterprises, primarily banks. As funds to the capital market evaporate and are withdrawn, the ability of other businesses to raise funds through this means is impaired. Where a cessation of speculation via equity ownership depresses share prices and drags down key indicators of capital market performance, the potential for negative feedback trading – the mirror image of the process that propelled prices upward initially – exacerbates the contraction of funds available through this means for naïve speculators.

While much of the discussion of distress arising out of the debt accumulated and the credit extended to finance the preceding speculation must proceed on the basis of the institutional features of the debt and equity contracts themselves, the story is incomplete without attention paid to the role of banks. In parallel fashion to the role of banks in the extension and creation of credit, in periods of distress, the contraction of credit through the banking system provides, or has the potential to provide, the main conduit through which distress spreads to other parts of the economy (see von Peter, 2004). Where banks respond through contracting broader credit, all businesses relying on bank credit to support and finance operations will be squeezed. The bank's portfolio of assets and liabilities are adversely affected by distress in the speculative markets directly if the bank credit has financed the speculation or the bank holds speculative assets, and indirectly, where portfolio spill-over occurs, as would be the case if a depressed speculative asset market depresses prices of substitutable assets which the bank holds or has a claim on. In 2000, for example, while the banks did not lend directly on NASDAQ-listed stocks, nor did they hold these assets directly, bank portfolios did include loans secured by real estate. With the collapse of the 'dot-com bubble', land values in California – the centre of the information technology industry – collapsed, which in turn depressed the book value of the west coast bank portfolios.

Initial shock (from declining investment returns and rising interest rates) is small relative to aggregate bank capital but does increase bank risk. Depositors and note holders convert bank debt to specie which banks meet by selling bonds, further depressing bond prices which, in turn, depresses the real values of bank loans to bond dealers collateralised by the bonds. Portfolio adjustment causes a drain in reserves that leads to a refusal by banks to rollover loans and the debt of brokers, forcing broker bankruptcy (Calomiris and Schweikart, 1991: 818–819 on the U.S. 1857 panic).

From this perspective, the length of time between the keynoting of the financial speculative activity and the revelation of the innovation's potential profitability critically influences the maximum duration of the mania. The longer the delay, the wider spread the impact of the innovation, the more intense the speculation and the greater the chance asset prices will be driven above any level that would be ultimately sustainable. In cases where extensive borrowing financed the prior speculation, the greater the revealed deviation of prices from fundamentals, the greater will be the distress. It is in this manner that the intensity of the prior speculation influences in a causal way the extent of the distress. Financial distress is alone a concern but not independent of the social distress. Compounding the downward spiral and motivating an exit from the speculative markets is the intrusion of pessimistic uncertainty and the gradual erosion of the attractions of fashion. As the innovation loses its novelty and becomes commonplace, the fashionable dimensions of it recede. Social differentiation is no longer possible and its benefits no longer yielded.[4] The norm of financial speculation proves transitory and its end creates a new uncertainty for indebted and naïve speculators – one characterised by worried concern and anxiety. Yet distress or anxiety is not the same thing as a panic.

Panic

Financial panic is the ill-advised, confused and uncoordinated scramble by speculators to dump shares quickly. It is both a personal emotion and a collective action that interfere critically with the preferred adaptive response to distress. The panic occurs in a demoralised environment created by the combination of the prevailing distress and a specific trigger. Like the mania, the panic is in every way a collective behavioural process. Unlike the mania, a clear, identifiable trigger sparks the panic and its hyper-intense life span is short.

Where once speculation was a norm of the collective – justified partly by the vague promise of the innovation – the end of the financial speculation is unexpected for many. 'When the norms of a group temporarily lose their efficacy as a guide to conduct, characteristic forms of collective behavior are likely to appear.'[5] For new and naïve speculators, the levelling off and gradual decline in the price of the speculative asset is unfamiliar. The result is demoralisation, 'the loss of meaningful relationship to the values and activities of some collectivity because changes in the balance of rewards make adherence no longer attractive' (Lang and Lang, 1962: 343–344).

More generally, the financial speculation emerged as a norm creating certainty where wider socio-economic uncertainty from the spreading impact of the innovation existed. The emergence of financial losses that threatens both investor solvency *and* reputation shatters recently created basic understandings and perceptions of the innovation-induced changes. The situation is now panic prone.

> As a collective process, demoralization entails disruption of two elements essential to the functioning of a group: *cognitive definitions* and *affective ties*. By cognitive definitions, we mean the patterns of expectations and intellectual schemes by which nature and society are transformed into a meaningful world. Persons become disoriented when the unexpected or unfamiliar shatters their basic understandings.... [W]hen

> external danger that cannot be mastered or internal dissension that cannot be resolved weakens the affective ties that normally weld people into a cohesive unit, it becomes panic-prone because of demoralization.
> (Lang and Lang, 1962: 346, original emphasis)

Without a trigger, however, it is possible for the demoralised state to evaporate. As prices stabilise, people readjust their perceptions of the financial situation and come to understand the nature of the changed socio-economic environment in which they exist and the threat of panic dissolves. Before readjustment is complete, however, if another event occurs to dramatically alter and adversely affect the tenuous security of the speculator – an event that serves to exaggerate the distress they face – it will trigger a panic.

In many documented historical instances of panic, the trigger was something that dramatically decreased the liquidity of the speculative assets. In October of 1929, for example, the sheer volume of American stock trading activity ran up against a technical trading barrier that, when hit, prevented the further execution of trades and reporting of price movements. In Thailand, when the monetary authorities floated the Thai baht, it altered instantly the terms of trade and liquidity characteristics of the speculative market. Any dramatic reduction in the liquidity of the speculative asset in a distressed environment will reasonably create heightened anxiety – for it was the liquid nature of the financial asset, in the presence of uncertain future gains, that encouraged the initial speculation. The trigger then might appear as a threshold level of activity that, when reached dramatically and quickly, constrains the asset's market liquidity. Alternatively, it may appear as some externally imposed change such as a government decree that alters either the terms of trade between the speculative asset and money or the ability to sell the asset at close to market price, such as was the case when Thailand let its currency float.

In a Schumpeterian manner, the mania will eventually end when society begins to perceive, and the economy begins to experience, the full potential of the innovation. As the economic fundamentals of the associated assets become increasingly predictable, the influence of fundamentals over asset prices reasserts itself. The resulting switching behaviour observed in asset price movements is consistent with the notion that speculators, reacting to such new information, begin to sell the speculative asset. The magnitude of the revealed deviation of contemporaneous prices from asset fundamentals may or may not be great. The resulting distress imposed upon indebted speculators may or may not be severe.

The proposed socio-economic explanation for panics suggests a material basis for incidences of financial, escape-mob behaviour. In a distressed environment, the onset of a panic requires a trigger. Given the importance of liquidity in providing some degree of perceived security against great losses, anything that causes a sudden and dramatic shift in the liquidity of the speculative asset will spark a panic.

By combining an economic perspective on financial instability with a sociological analysis of collective behaviour, this chapter lays out a conceptual foundation suggestive of a fuller understanding of extreme financial instability – speculative manias and financial panics. It offers a core conception of crises derivative of fundamental uncertainty and advanced financial capitalism. In the abstract, it suggests answers to who speculated in what, why, and how and in this way offers an explanation and a characterisation of the similarities in financial instability over time. In the absence of any better institutional definition, however, the framework remains too broad and too abstract to enlighten our understanding of the many variations historically observed.

Part III

Variations in manias, panics and crises

9 Societies in transition

Time–space comparisons of financial instability

Innovation drives the evolution of the capitalist system and the culture that is engendered ensures change will be perpetual. The nature of innovation is such that, at times, the induced social and economic changes are profound and profoundly uncertain. It is in these periods of major transition that the most spectacular of speculations – and recoil in crises – are most likely to occur. To the extent that there are recurring elements in this evolutionary process, there will be an enduring similarity of financial crises.

The socio-economic perspective adopted in this study incorporates an essential and explicit role for financial institutions in encouraging speculative accumulation and in fostering systemic instability. Where the nature of the contemporaneous innovation defines the focus of the preceding speculation, it is the particular constellation of financial institutions and the manner in which these institutions are integrated with the wider economy that give the episode its particular form. In these differences in the particular structure across time and space lie the source of the differences in historical crises – differences marked by the nature and focus of the distress and the manner and extent to which distress spreads to otherwise unrelated parts of the economy.

Historical financial systems consist of a variety of financial instruments, enterprises and processes that are designed to transfer purchasing power and that have evolved over time. The contemporary financial system offers such services as means of payment, the pricing of risk, portfolio allocation and the intermediation of such financial contract considerations as denomination, term, liquidity and the like designed to collect and promote accumulation of wealth. While the formal financial system, with its full complement of financial services, has a relatively recent history, constituent elements of the system have been in existence for centuries. Evidence of the use of coins as a medium of exchange and form of payment appear early in Western civilisation and even earlier in China, with some estimates dating the first use of coins to the twelfth century BC. Means of extending short-term credit to support trade and early risk-sharing arrangements afforded by such devices as marine insurance appear in medieval times. Italian moneychangers formed early currency markets in the twelfth century AD at cloth fairs that toured the Champagne and Brie regions of France. The bill of exchange, as a means of payment, was in use at this time as well.[1]

Whether intolerable inconvenience motivated these and other financial innovations or, as Paul Einzig (1966) argues, the innovations appeared as speculative improvements gaining a degree of acceptance before any 'impelling need for the reforms had arisen', the advantage of lower transactions cost goes some distance in aiding our understanding of a wide variety of financial developments. Money as a medium of exchange provides an intermediate link between the employment of resources to produce goods and services on the one hand and the ultimate consumption of those goods and services on the other. By valuing marketed commodities in money terms, the onerous task of negotiating the multitude of trading details associated with barter transactions is markedly reduced. Bills of exchange, as a complementary and derivative means of extending short-term trade credit, in addition to affording a means of payment, offer a similar convenience that further enhances trade.[2]

While early financial developments centred on the creation of processes and products designed to facilitate exchange and extend short-term trade credit, it was in the late seventeenth century that banks of issue and deposit, joint stocks and other institutions promoting the collection and allocation of private longer term savings began to play a noticeable role in Western European economies. It was not until the time of the Industrial Revolution, at the end of the eighteenth and into the first half of the nineteenth centuries that the formal financial system developed into a distinct industry comprised of all the basic enterprises, products and processes that define the contemporary financial structure in commercially and industrially advanced economies.[3] Such a long view of the evolution of the financial system suggests that its structure relates critically to the stage of contemporaneous economic development.

In broad strokes, as an economy develops in scale and scope, formal financial arrangements gradually (though incompletely) replace informal ones. As the economy's need for larger amounts of funds to finance larger capital projects rises, the increasing inefficiency of many informal financial systems yields to the efficiency of formal codified transactions. As Rondo Cameron and Hugh Patrick (1967: 1) observe,

> A proliferation of the number and variety of financial institutions and a substantial rise in the ratio of money and other financial assets relative to total output and tangible wealth are apparently universal characteristics of the process of economic development in market-oriented economies.

As societies become increasingly complex, the network of linkages created by the formal financial system expands and becomes more intricate. Yet, as a socio-economic process designed to render human interaction predictable – a process informed by local history and custom – its particular matrix of financial institutions varies in formal detail across predominantly capitalist societies at whatever the stage of economic development.

The remainder of this chapter revisits the crises that were sketched out at the beginning of this study as a way to consider in a brief, stylised manner the relationship between transitions across schematic stages of economic development and the corresponding degree of development of the formal financial system.[4] It alludes to a correspondence that existed between the extent of the crises occurring in these periods and the extent to which the contemporaneous financial systems supported the exchange of commodities and accumulation of material wealth. The purpose of the exercise is to provide an illustration of the sorts of considerations that might inform a more exhaustive analysis of any given crisis and to offer preliminary, if conjectural, support for an institutionally sensitive method of undertaking that analysis – a point I will explore in Chapter 10.

Early eighteenth-century English crises: transition to finance capitalism

In England's transition to what Joseph Schumpeter calls the 'capitalistic credit system' in the period preceding the 1720 crisis, there was a willingness to mobilise savings and to take risks in pursuit of profits. The agrarian landscape was undergoing radical transformation with the consolidation and enclosing of estates and the labourers as a conscious 'working class' was in the making.[5] The search for raw materials and markets for final products drove an outward-looking development policy and motivated colonial expansion. The formal financial system in its earliest periods of growth yielded banks and other institutional changes designed to mobilise financial capital to these ends.

Alexander Gerschenkron (1962) argues that England at the beginning of industrialisation required only small amounts of capital. With high concentrations of wealth and relatively small-scale investment opportunities, there was relatively little need for a formal financial system. As technology developed, the economy expanded, and the political centre of gravity moved to the nation state that was dominated by the wealthy few; the initial development of a formal financial system was sparked by the monarch's need to salvage its financial affairs. In late seventeenth- and early eighteenth-century England, the formal financial system developed around the state's need to raise revenue as a means of financing its exploits abroad. The creation of the Bank of England in 1694 marks the period in which the formal financial system as we know it today began to take shape. Over the preceding thirty years, through a 'complex series of hesitant steps', England saw the personal debt of the monarch transformed into a national debt under the control and management of Parliament. The Bank of England – a joint-stock bank initially owned by London's commercial interests – had as its primary purpose the financing of the state's imperial activities by taxation and the implementing of the permanent loan (Davies, 1994: 258–262).

The formal financial structure in the first quarter of eighteenth century was centred in London. A handful of joint-stock banks, one of which was the Bank of England, issued bank notes and supplied credit to large trading companies (primarily the East India and South Sea Companies).[6] Goldsmiths and scriveners provided London merchants with short-term credit in the form of discounted bills of exchange in addition to the circulating tallies and bank notes they provided.[7] The money supply was equally divided between these instruments and gold and silver coin.[8] Capital markets were insignificant and the remaining institutions such as insurance companies (offering property insurance primarily), savings banks and friendly societies (both with the principal function of alleviating poverty among the working classes) played only a residual role in the story that is central to this study. While it is common to suggest that the South Sea Bubble was directly and primarily the result of swindling and bribery, when viewed from a perspective of innovation and uncertainty, it appears less a tale of folly and more a lesson on the difficulties inherent in adjustment to innovation. As Neal (1990: 90; see also Garber, 1990) sees it

> A new financial system based on large-scale use of foreign bills of exchange, easily transferable shares of joint-stock corporations, and securely serviced long-term government debt grew up to accommodate the government's financial needs. But its inadequacies and innovational vigor led directly to the South Sea Bubble.

The English economy at this time was primarily an agricultural and artisan economy composed of a set of semi-autarkic local markets. On the collapse of the South Sea Bubble, England returned to its pre-bubble level of economic activity.[9] Julian Hoppit (1986: 45) argues that the limited geographical impact of the 1720 crisis can be explained by limited extent of the prior speculation.

> [The limited geographical impact] can be explained by the origins of the crises being restricted to the sphere of public finance; by the nature of the links between public and private finance which at the time were

relatively weak and poorly formed; and finally by the lack of integration nationally, which largely insulated private finance from a crisis of confidence on a large scale.

Although the bankruptcies were limited, the effects of the crisis and surrounding events on the financial structure were significant.[10] The path of financial development over the next century was one marked by an advanced development of private banking networks, an enhanced and critical role for private banking in the financing of commerce, and delayed development of capital markets. Government securities dominated the capital markets for the remainder of eighteenth century. Rondo Cameron (1967a) argues that the obstacles imposed by the requirement of a charter to operate a joint-stock company hindered the flow of equity capital to industry, thus forcing a greater reliance on the banks for working capital. This greater reliance on banks in default of a ready source of equity capital was instrumental in the development of an extensive banking network in this period. L.S. Pressnel (1956), in his detailed study of country banking, demonstrates the manner in which some industrialists entered banking so as to construct a source of longer term financing in the form of protracted short-term borrowing. In light of this history, it is perhaps unsurprising to find that banks play a central role in the future provision of speculative credit and the spreading of distress.

Early to middle nineteenth-century British crises: from take-off through a drive to maturity

By the mid-1800s, the British economy was in the middle stages of industrial development and experiencing commercial and financial crises with some regularity. International trade was of greater economic significance, more so than it had been in the earlier period. Technological change was transforming the manufacturing sector, increasing its relative economic importance. At the beginning of the century, the primary industries of agriculture, forestry and fishing accounted for one-third of the total estimated national income, while mining, manufacturing and building accounted for less than one-quarter. Over the next four decades, during which England experienced the full force of the Industrial Revolution, these proportions reversed themselves, with mining, manufacturing (cotton, iron and steam power), and building becoming the dominant industries (Deane and Cole, 1967; Neal, 1994). With the declining importance of Amsterdam as the European financial centre, Britain saw itself becoming the primary supplier of overseas credit which was promoted by the abolition of the many restrictions on foreign trade and gold movements in 1822.

National financial markets were in their early stages of development. Inter-provincial banking aided the movement of internationally traded goods to and from ports, and longer term funds financed investment in the infrastructure needed to support such movement. With the declining relative importance of specie and rising relative importance of bank money, by 1821, bank notes exceeded specie by a factor of approximately two to one (Cameron, 1967a: 42). In 1825, there were 715 banks – broadly categorised as London banks of deposit, discount and agency or country banks (Collins, 1991). Deposits linked country banks to agency banks in London and London banks to each other. The stock market in the first quarter of this century listed only shares of utilities and companies supplying the transportation infrastructure (waterworks and gas utilities, insurance, bridge, docks, road and canal companies) (Gayer *et al.*, 1975). The first railway line commenced operation from Darlington to Stockton in 1825. From 1827 through to 1836, five new railway companies were chartered each year (Kindleberger, 1984: 199) such that by 1840, railway stocks accounted for most of the corporate securities issued in England (Edwards, 1967 [1938]). The bond market continued, however, to consist of state debt almost exclusively.

John Stuart Mill (1967 [1826]) suggests that the expansion of credit to fuel speculation in this period came primarily from the practice of increasing the quantity and length of bills of exchange in addition to the extension of 'book credits' (accounts receivable).[11] As the Bank of England, and by association London bankers, would discount bills of no more than sixty-five days in length, the increased demand for longer terms stimulated the emergence of bill brokers. As specialists handling the negotiation of bills between London merchants in need of funds and country banks with surplus monies seeking temporary employment, this financial innovation formed the 'most distinctive and the most valuable institutional feature of the London money market' (Pressnel, 1956: 84 –85).

There was more widespread economic distress in the mid-1800s than there had been in the previous century. Two related features of the British economy that were not present in the 1700s may explain why. At its height, the 1825 mania encompassed not only the shares of Latin American mining companies but also the shares of most other publicly traded companies. In the 1840s, speculation centred on the novel railway developments, but the enthusiasm extended beyond the railroads to include other emerging industries, notably cotton. The subsequent collapse, then, affected several industries. Moreover, the integration of commodity and financial markets was more extensive, where 'the bulk of the evidence…testifies to the prominent role of credit in financing the Industrial Revolution' (Cameron, 1967a: 41 and 45). The crises spread from those institutions and companies directly involved with the primary speculations through the correspondent banking system to other markets in other regions. The result was that commercial activity otherwise unrelated to the speculation suffered from the contraction of credit.

Early twentieth-century American crisis: from the drive to maturity to high mass consumption

Formally, Walt Whitman Rostow (1990) defines maturity as the stage in which an economy demonstrates the capacity to move beyond the original industries that powered its take-off and to absorb and apply efficiently over a very wide range of its resources – if not the whole range – the most advanced fruits of modern technology. In the 'age of high mass consumption', leading sectors shift towards durable consumer goods and services. Real income per head rises to a point where a large number of persons gain a command over consumption that transcends basic food, shelter and clothing. The structure of the workforce changes with increases in the proportion of urban to total population and increases in the proportion of the population working in offices and at skilled factory jobs. Resources tend increasingly to be directed to consumer durables and to the diffusion of services on a mass basis. Historically, we can observe this shift in the transition from the coal, iron and heavy engineering industries of the railway phase to machine tools, chemicals, and electrical equipment in both Britain and the United States in the late nineteenth century and early twentieth centuries. 'It was a period of rapid improvement in transportation and communication facilities, of relatively free trade, and of large-scale migration of both capital and people' (Cameron, 1972: 3).

By the 1920s, the American economy had developed all the structural and market features of a contemporary industrialised economy. Agriculture was well on the way from the multi-crop family farm to a system of large and specialised operations, accounting for one-quarter of the total national income. Manufacturing was well established and expanding, aided by recent technological advances in chemical, electrical and machine technologies. The early twentieth-century American financial system included all of the basic institutions and markets that comprise the modern-day one. The stock markets listed and traded daily the stocks of corporations from a wide variety of industries; the bond market listed debt instruments of a variety of private and public enterprises; and investment banking services had become institutionalised so that portfolio considerations, rather than colonial trade considerations, guided international capital flows.

Credit to finance the speculation came directly from the call-loan market. As a direct reflection of the extent of speculation supported by margin trading, the call-loan volume rose from $3 billion in 1927 to more than

$8.5 billion by September of 1929, in part fuelled by the recycling through the call-market funds obtained from newly floated securities (Snyder, 1930). Suppliers of funds to the call-loan market were primarily New York City banks and foreign banking agencies (Board of Governors, 1943: 434). Call loans formed the principal secondary reserve asset for banks (Thomas, 1935) and brokers' loans comprised almost 50 per cent of the loan portfolio of New York City banks (Board of Governors, 1943). Banks accommodated a shift in corporations' demand from bank loans to securities and investment banking services by creating the securities affiliate. Bank participation in the distribution of new equity issues increased from 37 per cent of the total distribution in 1927 to more than 60 per cent by 1930 (Carosso, 1970).

The level of economic integration in the United States at this time was dramatically greater than it had been in either of the earlier two English periods. The relative domestic and international importance of the American manufacturing sector was greater. The manufacturing industries now relied heavily on the capital markets for funds. Links between financial-centre banks and the stock and bond markets were solid, created directly by the existence of stocks and bonds in bank portfolios and indirectly through both the bank securities' affiliates and loans for which stocks formed the collateral. Inter-bank deposits linked financial-centre banks with smaller regional banks, and international capital flows united financial-centre banks around the world. The result was that an increased proportion of national income from any one market relied heavily on the proper functioning of the other markets. Problems in one sector reverberated through the financial system causing and compounding problems in other sectors.

The American stock market was a weak link. Its collapse adversely affected the manufacturing sector's ability to raise capital. Falling stock prices weakened the securities affiliates of financial centre banks whose portfolios included stocks and threatened the solvency of others for which stocks formed loan collateral (Kaufman, 1995). The weakness spilled over to the smaller regional banks when funds moved to the money-centre banks in the attempt to offset the impending threat to liquidity. Withdrawals from correspondent banks, worried depositors, and foreign holders of US dollars all exerted an unsustainable pressure on liquidity. The attempt to bolster liquidity by selling off existing securities sparked a downward debt-deflation spiral. Additional stress imposed first by the agricultural depression on poorly diversified unit banks (White, 1983) and later by an international monetary crisis could not be withstood. The general contraction of credit that the bank failures produced further depressed economic activity.[12]

Although the Federal Reserve System, through rediscounting, had the ability to act as a lender of last resort, a significant proportion of the troubled banks were not members. Consequently, the Federal Reserve took no responsibility for the performance of these banks. Such inaction leads many to conclude that the severity of the problems could have been avoided with better central-bank management (Friedman and Schwartz, 1963: 270, for example).

In the wake of the crash, several regulatory changes appeared. Federal securities regulators introduced the 'blue sky' laws that required 'full and fair disclosure of the character of securities' and issuers to file a detailed statement of this character with the newly created Securities Exchange Commission (Carosso, 1970: 356). The Bank Act of 1933 (the 'Glass–Steagall Act') legislated a temporary system of deposit insurance – which became permanent with the 1935 creation of the Federal Deposit Insurance Corporation – and imposed the separation of investment from retail banking. The legal separation remained in force until its repeal with the 1999 Financial Services Modernization Act.

Late twentieth-century American crises: from high mass consumption to the information age

In the late twentieth century, the American economy was in the midst of a transition to what some have called the information age. An increasing number of businesses in all industries were becoming dependent on the computer as a means of storing, processing and delivering information. By the end of the century, personal computers, together with the Internet, were fast becoming a household necessity. The technology was altering (and continues to alter) all manner of economic and social interaction.

Speculation in the clusters of advances that mark the revolution in information and communications was itself affected by the innovations. The innovations that defined the focus of the speculation and the advances altered the manner in which people speculated. Trading directly in the stocks of Internet, computer hardware and software companies was itself mediated by the computer. The enhanced processing of data and the greater ease of access to that data fuelled an enthusiasm that propelled the NASDAQ index upwards, gathering an ever-greater number of investors. At its peak, it is estimated that nearly 50 per cent of Americans were participating in the stock market.[13]

The late twentieth-century American financial structure had essentially the same network of institutions supplying financial services as those that had existed seventy years earlier, but their operations were substantially more sophisticated and important but subtle shifts were occurring. Portfolio and risk management benefited from the advanced processing of information that computers afforded and better management benefited from the stability of retail and investment banking operations alike. Stock market trading was active, widespread and accessible to not only financial institutions such as the investment banking firms and pension funds but also to non-financial corporations and individuals. The relative importance of intermediated funds transfers was yielding to the accessibility of the direct markets. The Federal Reserve had been actively operating as a provider of emergency liquidity for decades.

While the collapse of the 'dot-com bubble' resulted in a slowdown in the economy, the slowdown was short lived and nowhere near as devastating as the 1929 experience. In its effort to counter the contractionary effects of the crash, the American central bank cut short-term interest rates by almost five percentage points in 2001. The action successfully offset the balance sheet effects of loan losses on the banks' portfolios and 'spurred a rapid increase in core deposits, which provided banks with plentiful, low-interest rate funding' (Bassett and Carlson, 2002: 259). The Fed-driven combination of lower interest rates and additional liquidity ensured that despite the economic slowdown, the US commercial banking industry remained solvent and profits remained high in 2001. This action combined with a smaller portion of the commercial economy relying on the banking system for credit helped to contain the depressing effects of the crash largely to the industries related to the initial advance.

Late twentieth-century emerging market crises: transitions of a different sort

In late twentieth-century Eastern European and Asian countries, the transition appeared in the conversion from a centralised political structure, with industrial development and financing directed by the nation state, to an increasingly diffuse market-oriented system. Innovation as it affected these societies appeared less in the form of internally induced technological change leading to industrialisation and more in the form of economic and political restructuring. An outward looking development policy focused not on importing cheap raw materials but rather on attracting relatively cheap funds for internal development and adoption of foreign technologies. The need for foreign exchange to service the foreign debt drove the search for external markets in which to sell final goods and services produced.

Prior to the mid-1980s, a cartel of four to five major banks dominated Thailand's major sectors.[14] As centres of 'sprawling business conglomerates', the banks dominated first agri-business, then import-substituting consumer industries and basic process industries and finally urban services. In addition to Japanese foreign direct investment, these banks supplied the bulk of funds to support capital formation. Close links between the business leaders and the politicians ensured the protection of the bank cartel until the 1980s energy crisis forced Thailand to adopt the World Bank's export-oriented development strategy in exchange for temporary financial assistance. With this external intervention came a 'transfer of power over economic policy making into the hands of technocrats' and, in the 1990s, a push to liberalise the financial system. In 1990, restrictions on convertibility were removed; in 1993, an offshore banking facility was established to enable foreign lenders to lend in the Thai market. In the same period, stock market rules changed to attract foreign investors, and encouraging Thailand's direct access to foreign funds diminished the bank cartel's influence. Capital inflows surged. While portfolio investments increased, the vast majority of the new funds arrived in the form of loans. Private-sector foreign debt increased tenfold. By 1996, Thailand's foreign debt was equal to approximately 70 per cent of the Thai GDP, with over 60 per cent of the total held in the private sector.

Over this period, investment in agriculture declined, rural population migrated to the urban centres and the export mix shifted from cheap labour industries, such as textiles, to technology-based industries including computer parts, auto parts and electrical goods. Multi-national companies controlled the technology and focused on development for export, while domestic conglomerates focused on property development, services (finance, retail and media) and infrastructure (roads, telecommunications and power generation). From 1993 onwards, foreign loans financed the domestic expansion, particularly in property development and telecommunications.

With a pegged currency and a newly liberalised capital account, the government soon lost control of the macro-economy. To prevent overheating, the monetary authorities raised interest rates with every intention of restricting liquidity and slowing the rapid growth. In the era of free flowing 'hot money', however, the higher rates served only to attract more financial inflows in form of short-term liquid loans denominated in foreign currencies – at the peak, more than 60 per cent of the foreign loans held a maturity of less than one year. The percentage of short-term foreign debt to foreign exchange reserves was well over 100 for the two years prior to the crisis in Thailand (see Ghosh, 2001: 82).

The substantial drop in the external value of the Thai currency combined with the distress that had spread to all sectors of the economy created a fire-sale opportunity. Foreign direct investment again rose to dominate capital inflows through 1998 and 1999, but this time it was not for new investment but to acquire cheap assets. At the beginning of 1997, Thailand had fifteen commercial banks and ninety-two finance companies; three years later, twenty-three finance companies remained in operation and all but the largest five banks had been closed, whose assets were transferred to the government's Krung Thai Bank or sold to foreign financial interests.

The foreign take over in other industries, notably export, retail and telecommunications industries, saw Thai ownership lost to Japanese, American and continental European business interests. Financial liberalisation destroyed the Asian form of entrepreneurial banking with potentially serious consequences for future national development. As Pasuk Phongpaichit and Chris Baker (2000: 228–229) argue,

> The international banks are likely to favour international firms because the systems and relationships are already in place. They will concentrate on consumer banking and risk management, where they have clear advantages through technology and experience. They are much less likely to take over the Thai banks' old role of funding ambitious entrepreneurship on the basis of personal relationships and personal market knowledge.[15]

Summary and conclusion

Each stage of economic and financial development involves a relationship between broad classes of factors. Resources, population, technology, social institutions (government, religion and the educational system, for example) and concentration of wealth combine to shape the economy's need for an institutionalised supply of financial capital. The path of development from an agricultural economy comprised of semi-autarkic local markets to an industrially and commercially advanced economy passes through a variety of stages. In broad strokes, these stages will involve in some way the introduction of large-scale industrial production for mass consumption offering an increasingly diverse array of consumer goods and the enlargement of an urban workforce providing labour to the large-scale production and an expanding service sector. The paths of development will differ across societies, however, and no one detailed schematic of stages could adequately reflect the variations in these paths. Rather, acknowledging the path-dependent nature of both the innovations that propel a society forward and the broad set of socio-economic institutions created to manage and adapt in everyday life implies that any fuller analysis must attend to these important institutional and hence society-specific details.

If history matters – and the fundamental premise of this study is that it does – an understanding of the differences in crises demands first an understanding of the evolution of the society-specific relationship between these broad classes of factors in a given society *over* time. To this end, the juxtaposition of the eighteenth- and nineteenth-century English episodes as well as the twentieth-century American episodes afforded such an illustrative comparison. At the beginning of the eighteenth century, England was in the early stages of transition to a system of capitalism with the economy comprised largely of a set of semi-autarkic local markets. A century later, England was securing her place as the leader in the supply of overseas credit; mining and manufacturing were quickly becoming the dominant domestic industries, with larger scale production in manufacturing requiring the rapid expansion of factory workers located in urban areas. Increased specialisation served to integrate the economy facilitated by a parallel development in the financial structure and its networks. In the first quarter of the twentieth century, the United States was in the later stages of growth and transition into a period of high mass consumption. By the end of the century, the American economy was in the throes adapting to revolutionary changes in information and communication technologies. The later advances affected both the financial and non-financial economic activity. The financial structure, while functionally the same in these two periods, had undergone profound changes in the last quarter of the twentieth century.

By way of a different example, the twentieth-century Thailand crisis was considered. Thailand throughout the 1980s experienced some elements of growth consistent with the stages of take off and drive to maturity (to use Rostow's labels), driven less by internal technological advance and more by the rapid adoption of external technologies introduced through foreign direct investment. At the beginning of the transition in the early 1980s, the Thai economy was still predominantly agricultural, with this industry employing nearly 70 per cent of the workforce. Throughout the transition over the next decade and a half, Thailand experienced substantial migration of labour from the rural areas to the urban centres of manufacturing, with employment in these industries encompassing nearly half of the labour force by the mid-1990s.

As an economy advances, capital projects become larger, wealth becomes less concentrated and the need for a formal financial system – comprised of financial markets and formal financial enterprises as the centres in which funds transfers occur – increases.

> The number and variety of financial institutions and a substantial rise in the ratio of money and other financial assets relative to total output and tangible wealth are apparently universal characteristics of the process of economic development in market-oriented economies.
>
> (Cameron and Patrick, 1967: 1)

The gradual diffusion of wealth and the participation of a greater number of people require legal financial contracts governing the terms of the transfer, with the trust and loyalty embedded in kinship ties replaced by exchanges between unknown principals. In Thailand, the rapid externally stimulated economic transition was not matched by a comparable transition in internal customs. Juxtaposed against the alleged objectivity of foreign financial institutions, the kinship ties defining the informal Thai networks appeared subjective and corrupt.[16]

In the earliest stages of development of this formal financial structure, we see a primacy of rudimentary financial instruments (bank notes, bills of exchange) over financial intermediaries.[17] As economies move into the early to middle stages of development, we see a primacy of financial institutions over financial markets as reflected in a relatively high proportion of funds moving through formal financial institutions. Although the ultimate saver and the ultimate use of the funds may not know each other in this transition from relationship exchanges to purely and exclusively anonymous ones defined by market transfer, the system will pass through an intermediate stage involving personal contact with those who can mediate the transfer. In eighteenth-century England, the development of formal financial institutions was an outgrowth and extension of the familiar business that goldsmiths, attorneys and scriveners were performing. As the complexity of the financial linkages continued to develop in step with the complexity of the economy, financial transactions moved outside the financial enterprises into the markets executing direct financial transactions. Later advances in information technology promoted the development of financial instruments and, thus, the markets for financial instruments, such that there has been a marked decline in the relative importance of the financial intermediary over recent years.[18]

Through the mid to later stages of financial development, we see a decline in the relative importance of formal financial institutions in the transfer of funds. As financial instruments developed, aided significantly by the advancements in calculation and the like afforded by computational advances, and with it markets for their direct exchange, funds transfers are increasingly executed directly in specialised markets, bypassing the intermediary. If this is indicative of a general trend, as the economies move into the mid to later stages of development, we will see a higher proportion of income and wealth held in financial instruments but a lower proportion of those instruments held in financial institutions as compared with the earlier stages of development.

Although limited, this comparison of episodes – separated not only geographically and temporally but also by degree of economic development – suggests that the degree of economic and financial integration may be a factor in the transmission of financial distress. With expanded networks of greater intricacy comes the increased number of channels through which distress might spread. Systemic risk, or the possibility that a financial crises will depress activity in otherwise unrelated markets, seems to be greater the more closely and directly linked are financial and aggregate economic activity.

To prevent widespread distress, many have argued for the critical presence of a lender of last resort. This brief comparison suggests that to prevent the primary source of crisis in speculative objects, there is a need for a buyer of last resort in the critical asset markets.[19] If the secondary distress is dependent on the degree of integration afforded by the financial system, then the critical importance of this policy response derives from the extent to which the financial networks are integrated and how they are integrated with the wider economy. Where economies are not well integrated, as in 1720 England, the distress will remain contained. As the economies become more integrated through the networks of financial institutions supplying credit to a wider variety of economic activity, containment is achieved through the actions of a lender of last resort.

This brief comparison is suggestive of a complex multi-faceted relationship between crises, the financial structure and the economy. Such complexity leaves us predisposed to accept the hypothesis of Cameron (1967a) and others that the functional–structural relationship between the financial system and the economy involves a two-way causality.[20] The financial system shapes and is shaped by the stage of economic development at a point in time, and the manner in which the financial system evolves over time shapes and is shaped by the particular evolution of the economy. These relationships, in turn, inform the nature and evolution of historical crises. Where the stage of development in the real and financial sectors shed light on the differences in historical crises, we also see hints – in the legislative responses to and ownership changes after at least three of six crises discussed – of the way in which the crises themselves can shape the future evolution of the financial system. The next challenge is to explore a means of representing these networks in a way that promotes greater consistency in analysis.

10 The bottom line

Towards institutional indicators of financial fragility

The highly stylised comparison of these six sample crises occurring over time and across countries is suggestive of a complex relationship between episodes of crises and the underlying structure of both the economy and its financial system. While the broad similarities across episodes are derivative of the drive to accumulate and innovate in a financial capitalist system wherein credit may be endogenously created to support and promote such speculation, observed differences in crises stem from the differences in the specific economic and financial structure in which the particular episode occurs. Characteristic differences in the unfolding of these and other episodes include differences in the industrial or sectoral location of the initial innovation, the particular source and nature of the credit extended to support the speculation, the manner in and extent to which credit is endogenously created and the extent to and manner in which the precipitating speculation or subsequent distress spread to persons and spheres of economic activity otherwise unrelated to the initial innovation.

The formal financial structure consists of various financial instruments, processes and legal enterprises. The financial structure varies over time and across nations in terms of the relative size and economic importance of these broad classes of constituent elements. As a set of institutions, the financial structure evolves over time in response to a variety of economic, technological and other institutional changes. The structure of a nation's economy will shape the financing needs of a nation, as we have seen in Chapter 9. Innovation and technological changes can affect both the nature of the financial contract defining the terms of funds transfer and the processes by which the transfer occurs. And the legal system, as a separate institutional structure, influences the shape and structure of the financial system through its treatment of property rights, shareholder protections and creditor entitlements generally, and the characteristics of the financial contracts specifically.[1]

To understand more fully the evolving nature of financial crises we require a more detailed elaboration of the functional importance of the financial system located in the evolving historical economies and the changing financial structures in which they occur. If we wish to better understand the varied nature of crises, we need a means of mapping the varied economic and financial detail defined by dominant sectors and specific financial institutions. We seek, in other words, a representation that will enable a better understanding of the historical economy as one comprised of sectors and industries linked to and through the broader financial networks. If successful and practicable, such a representation could well afford a means of systematically comparing how crises can vary from economy to economy – how the 1997 Asian crisis was both similar to yet different from the crisis occurring in the wake of the 1720 South Sea Bubble.

The objective of this chapter is to consider one such means by which the financial structure may be more fully represented so as to afford a systematic comparison of some of the quantifiable relations consistent with this perspective on the financial crisis-structure relationship. At its most basic of levels, the economic issues suggested by the earlier discussion and characterisation of the speculation-crisis phenomenon are portfolio issues. The original source of the innovation and speculation translates into a rebalancing of portfolios in favour of related financial assets. The structure and extent of credit in relation to the monetary value of non-financial assets of the innovation determine the financial 'health' of a given portfolio and thus the portfolio's ability to withstand shocks. The spread of distress depends critically on the network of financial assets and liabilities created by interlocking sectoral portfolios. Accordingly, the systematic means of evaluating the source, impact and transmission of distress that defines historical crises in a manner that permits assessment of the systemic threat of a given crisis lies, in the first instance, in the details potentially revealed in a nation's balance sheet and the evolution of the asset–liability matrix over a specific crisis episode.

The economic and social devastation caused by the Mexican, South East Asian, Argentinean, Russian and Brazilian crises of the 1990s prompted an international effort to develop a more robust set of prudential indicators of financial soundness.[2] Seeking indicators that move beyond the institution-specific indicators of financial soundness represented by the CAMELS framework, international financial agencies (most notably the International Monetary Fund, the Bank for International Settlements, the European Central Bank, the Organisation for Economic Co-operation and Development and the World Bank) through both concerted and independent efforts have been developing and testing the efficacy of macroprudential indicators as early warning signals.[3] As with the CAMELS indicators, the vast majority of the postulated macroprudential indicators are either directly balance sheet indicators or indicators whose influence on financial soundness works directly through their effect on a sector's balance sheet (such as price, currency or interest rate volatility). It is not until recently, however, that attempts have been guided by a systematic and coherent attempt to locate the search for indicators in the context of developing the nation's balance sheet (see, e.g. Allen *et al.*, 2002; IMF, 2004; Organisation for Economic Co-operation and Development, 2004).[4]

Depending on how the data are or will be compiled in accordance with the System of National Accounts standards, they could provide a link between the financial sector and other sectors in the economy. Diversity in financial institutions, the instruments these institutions use, accounting rules, practices and reporting methods employed, combined with the fact that these data are published annually with substantial delay continue to produce significant obstacles to the usefulness of the data (IMF, 2001; see Organisation for Economic Co-operation and Development, 2004).[5] These limitations are significantly binding for examining the details which this study proposes would usefully inform a more detailed study of crises. Since most crises evolve over periods much shorter than one year, the best we can do at this point is to conjecture about the information that might be revealed were the data available at a higher frequency and identify some of the additional benefits of such information as a means of encouraging international efforts in this endeavour.

The foremost benefit of a full set of balance sheet relations is the potential it holds to reflect financial structural differences across nations and changes over time.[6] At the present time, the majority of indicators proposed have been tested against their ability to assess the soundness of contemporary financial systems and forewarn only recent crises. The refinement of prudential indicators guided by an *ex post* assessment of recent experience alone suggests we remain exposed to the risk that as the economies and financial systems continue to evolve, the indicators slip in relative importance as useful indicators of systemic financial fragility. By conceptually seeking to map the full range of portfolio connections, we would have a basis against which to refer structural changes and thus have at our disposal a means by which to gauge such future financial developments; and we would have a comprehensive and coherent means of consistently *approaching* the selection of indicators of financial soundness relevant to a nation's state of financial (and economic) development flexible enough to accommodate financial evolution.

This chapter seeks to frame the importance of balance sheet indicators in a context that permits a more flexible structural–functional perspective.[7] It interprets a nation's asset–liability matrix in the context of an adaptation and extension of Raymond Goldsmith's (1969) analysis of financial structure and economic development. Subsequent work by Ross Levine (1997) and others have explored refinements to Goldsmith's basic hypothesis that the level of economic development is functionally dependent on the development and structure of the financial system.[8] Their analyses, as does Goldsmith's, employ only highly aggregated indicators of the financial structure. More recently, Joseph P. Byrne and E. Philip Davis (2003) undertake a cross-country comparison of sectoral financing behaviour in OECD countries.[9] Viewed from the perspective of the development–financial structure nexus, Byrne and Davis are disaggregating the Goldsmith–Levine framework. Viewed from the perspective of portfolio stability, they are extending the balance sheet analysis beyond the traditional areas of household assets and corporate liabilities to include all major sectors of the economy. In this way, the resulting balance sheet of assets and liabilities is viewed as an application of the structural representation suggested earlier by Goldsmith.

These recent extensions offer insight and guidance into the way in which one might interpret and analyse the nation's balance sheet for examining the speculation-crisis phenomenon generally and its systemic elements specifically. The domino distress effect – where distress in one part of the financial system *creates* distress in another part of the system, then in otherwise unrelated parts of the economy – essentially defines the 'systemic' nature of a crisis and derives from a few broad relationships.[10] At its most aggregated of levels, the extent to which the economy relies on the formal financial system to support and promote economic activity determines the relative importance of formal financing and thus the extent to which a system failure will adversely affect different parts of the wider economy. The extent to which the formal financial system experiences distress as a result of distress of any one set of institutions within the system depends, in turn, on the relative importance of the particular set of institutions, the extent of concentration within that set and the extent to which the financial and non-financial enterprises and markets are linked through portfolio networks to that distressed set of institutions. Traditionally, the financial structure has been broadly differentiated on the basis of a dominance of either intermediated or marketed funds transfer (see Allen and Gale, 1995, and Demirgüç-Kunt and Levine, 2001, for example). Systemic risks within the respective sets of institutions (intermediaries or markets) derive from the extent to which a few firms dominate the subsector, or how closely connected the respective portfolios are or both.

In the case where portfolio links define the systemic fragility of the financial system, we need to look beyond the broad, highly aggregated indicators of financial structures to the more disaggregated information that only the sectoral balance sheets have the potential to reveal. Disaggregating national balance sheet information has the potential to expose the network of linkages that inform and define the underlying sector-specific fragilities. By identifying sector financing behaviour for all major sectors of the economy, the disaggregation permits an examination of who financed whom, what and how in institutionally specific detail. Disaggregating sector portfolios further by such characteristics as term to maturity and currency denomination can reveal emerging fragilities as the prior speculation and subsequent distress unfold. Combined, the national balance sheet, disaggregated by sector and by financial characteristics, has the potential to expose evolution of inherent systemic fragilities created by the society's specific network of financial linkages in a manner that could promote consistent comparisons across historical episodes. To be as clear as possible, we are seeking to identify differences in financial structures as reflected in a comparison of portfolios of assets and liabilities where these differences appear across nations due to the varying nature of the underlying economies in which crises occur, and over time due to the effects of the unfolding of a given speculation-crisis phenomenon.

Evolving financial systems

Goldsmith (1969) defines the evolution of the financial system in terms of the relative sizes of financial instruments, enterprises, degree of concentration, relation of the volume of financial instruments and of the funds held in financial institutions. He captures the relationship between the financial structure and the underlying level of economic development by comparing these financial indicators to the relevant economic magnitudes of national wealth, national product, capital formation and savings.

> The differences among countries in financial development are reflected in the changes in the quantitative and qualitative relations between the size and character of the financial superstructure on the one hand, and of the infrastructure of national wealth and national product, on the other. ...[I]mportant characteristics of the financial structure of a country during a given period are reflected in the distribution of total financial flows among instruments and among sectors; in the share of financial institutions in the transactions in financial instruments, in the aggregate and by type; and in the distribution of total financial transactions of the various sectors and subsectors among different financial instruments.
>
> (Goldsmith, 1969: 29)

The economy's reliance on the formal financial structure

The financial system provides basic services of payments, collection of savings and allocation of investments. The fact that the system can create credit as well introduces a source of instability that, when paired with optimistic uncertainty of the type encouraged by the adoption and adaptation to a revolutionary innovation, creates the potential for instability to become acute. When the institutions of the financial system fail, the system itself fails to provide even the basic financial services. Financial networks determine and define the channels through which distress spreads out from the financial sector to other non-financial spheres of the economy. The threat of a systemic crisis derives from the risk that the loss of these services and withdrawal of credit interferes with the normal non-financial operations of the economy.

Failure of the system to offer a medium of exchange and payments services will result in the need to devote greater resources to the mere function of exchange than would otherwise be the case.[11] The more an economy relies on the institutionalised supply of a uniform medium of exchange in order to effect exchange, the more it will suffer in the wake of a collapse of the institution(s) supplying the media. Indeed, the worst crises appear to be those that have resulted in a sudden and dramatic decline in access to short-term funds for immediate and near-term commercial transaction purposes.[12]

Historically, issuers of the media of exchange have included governments, public banks, commercial banks, goldsmiths and other private individuals engaged in commerce. Adopting the portfolio perspective insofar as assets and liabilities are concerned, the issuance of 'money' as a liability entails an asset acquired in exchange. These assets could be (have historically been) loan contracts for a variety of purposes, such as providing working capital to commercial enterprises and operating funds to the government. Alternatively, the assets could be stocks in a trading company, as was the case in eighteenth-century England. In the case of the collapse of the South Sea Bubble, the adverse effect on the associated economies was limited. Contrariwise, an economy that relies more heavily on the institutionalised supply of commercial credit to finance a significant portion of its economic activity will suffer comparatively much more in the wake of institutional collapse.

As with those media that facilitate the exchange of consumption goods in a single period framework, financial assets and liabilities have the potential to enable effectively and efficiently the transfer of purchasing power over time. The failure of either the issuing institutions or a collapse in the associated markets designed to exchange the instruments of exchange will threaten the proper functioning of the multi-period economy. Most notably, the investment so financed is at risk of being adversely affected. Logically, the extent of the wider economic impact will be a function of the degree to which real economic activity is dependent on the funds rendered accessible by such instruments and services. The more an economy depends on investment financed by the formal financial system, the more the economy will suffer in the wake of an institutional or market collapse that disrupts the transfer of loanable funds.

Medium of exchange instruments have traditionally been government-issued currency liabilities circulating outside banks and bank-deposit liabilities. As such, traditional measures of the money supply, as a constituent element of total-system liabilities and as a proportion of Gross Domestic Product (GDP), are indicators of the functional importance of the media of exchange in the economic activity. The potential of these media of exchange instruments for moving outside the traditional payments system due to recent advances in information and communications technologies, however, may threaten the usefulness of this measure in the not-so-distant future. To the extent that private sector non-financial firms offer credit with broader purchasing power – such as credits with telecommunications companies used to pay for small-value retail purchases of consumer goods – the traditional measures of the money supply risk becoming obsolete and with it their usefulness as indicators of relative financial importance (see, e.g. King, 1999 and Visano, 2002). Thus, looking forward, revisions to such an indicator might be necessary for assessing the functional importance of the media of exchange instruments.

Aggregate indicators of structural–functional dependence

Degree of financial development

The degree of formal financial development is an important constituent element in any characterisation of a country's financial superstructure. One set of measures of financial 'depth' derives from measures of the money supply as a proportion of national income. Although widely available for most countries, and useful for ascertaining the relative financial importance of deposit-taking enterprises, such metrics serve a limited purpose in characterising overall financial development. Yet by measuring only those sets of financial instruments designed primarily to provide transactions services, these measures exclude those instruments whose primary function is to channel funds from savers to investors and other net users of funds and indicate nothing at all of an economy's wider credit creation possibilities.

As a complementary indicator, Ross Levine favours total private sector credit to national income as the preferred measure of financial depth or development.[13] Allowing for the historical possibility that public credit is at least as important as private sector credit in financing innovation and given the fact that the risk of crisis lies in the entire set of spheres comprising the formal financial system, it is the broadest measure of financial development that is the preferred measure for the purpose at hand. At the most aggregated of levels, then, it is the market value of the stock of total financial liabilities and share equity outstanding as a percentage of GDP that best captures a society's degree of financial development. This most aggregated of indicators accounts for all credit instruments and share equity and as such is an overall indicator of the extent to which the economy relies on a formal financial system to execute transfers of funds.

Degree of financial intermediation

The extent to which the economy relies on intermediated funds is a second critical element in any characterisation of a country's financial structure. The degree of financial intermediation, in comparison with its overall degree of financial development, will yield important information about the extent of indirect versus direct financing and, consequently, the relative economic importance of bank-based versus market-based sources of funds.

> One of the most important characteristics of a country's financial structure and development is the extent to which the issues of domestic non-financial and of foreign issues are absorbed or held by domestic financial institutions rather than by domestic non-financial sectors or by foreigners particularly domestic households. It is this relation which reflects the degree of institutionalization in the country's financial structure and the relative importance of direct and indirect financing.
>
> (Goldsmith, 1969: 317)

While much of recent banking theory supports (or is, at least, not antithetical to) the notion that there exists a complementarity between bank-aided and market-executed funds transfers, overall the theory all but exclusively holds that banks as intermediaries offer services that aid portfolio allocation and remains silent on the credit-creation function of banks (see Chapter 7). By creating and managing credit and, more importantly, by creating and managing what is, in most economies, the primary means of payment, banks play a significant role in the unfolding of a financial crisis, a role that is central in determining the extent to which a localised financial crisis does or does not spill over into the wider economy. As such, identifying the extent to which an economy relies on intermediation through the primary deposit-creation institutions is essential in adapting the structural framework for examining the evolution of crises. An adaptation of Goldsmith's (1969: 317) Financial Intermediation Ratio might be adopted for this purpose and would be determined by dividing the market value of total liabilities and share equity issued by domestic deposit-taking financial institutions at a given date by the total value of all liabilities outstanding. To differentiate it from Goldsmith's original ratio, it is referred here to as the Bank Intermediation Ratio.

The relative economic importance of intermediated versus marketed supplies of funds – identified implicitly by comparing the degree of financial development with the degree of financial intermediation – determines the relative importance of the particular set of financial institutions. Financial system distress emanating from either of these two groups depends, in turn, on the degree of concentration within each group and the extent to which portfolios are linked across the two broad groups and to the other non-financial sectors in the economy.

Financial concentration

Beyond the degree of financial intermediation is the degree of concentration as a measure of the relative importance of a given set of institutions or markets in servicing the overall financial needs of the economy.[14] Taking the liability concentration ratio (as the balance sheet counter part to the asset concentration ratio) for the four or five largest banks, yields an indicator of structure by quantifying the extent to which deposit-taking institutions form either a closely or loosely concentrated financial network. The ratio of total financial liabilities of the largest four or five deposit institutions as a percentage of total financial liabilities held in deposit banks augments the bank intermediation ratio by indicating the relative economic importance of the four or five largest financial intermediaries. Together, the financial concentration ratio and the bank intermediation ratio offer a snapshot of the relative economic importance of a nation's largest banks in financing overall economic activity.[15]

A clarification is in order before proceeding further. It is recognised that there is scope to claim a greater stability of larger financial institutions. Much of the argument in favour of this position hinges on the greater opportunities for achieving adequate portfolio diversification as afforded by the larger asset base. The importance of this consideration is neither denied nor refuted.[16] Rather, the argument here is *if* a given financial institution fails, the systemic impact will be greater the larger the institution and will be greater the more closely networked to other financial institutions.

As such, these two elements identify potential sources of impact and transmission effects and parallel what the Group of Ten call 'width' and 'depth' of a shock.[17]

Benjamin Sahel and Jukka Vesala (2001: 182–183) writing for the Bank of International Settlements, capture well the necessary distinctions.

> Large banks may have a more diversified portfolio of activities, especially when the whole banking group is taken in to consideration. But although the likelihood that large banks will incur major problems might be lower, the impact of such problems occurring at a large bank would be more widespread. Absolute size is not the only relevant factor, however. The interbank market is a major channel for contagion. Contagion may also spread through capital market activities or through difficulties experienced at non-bank subsidiaries. This being the case, structural features – such as the ownership structure or composition of the group or conglomerate to which the bank belongs – might also provide an indication of the systemic importance of the bank. A particular bank might be a core intermediary in a particular market, even if it does no rank among the largest institutions.

In other words, a larger financial enterprise in a more consolidated financial system might well be able to better withstand a shock of a given magnitude at a point in time as compared to a smaller financial firm in a less consolidated system (see Group of Ten, 2001: Chapter 3). But *when* the larger institution fails, the systemic risk to the economy and the nation is much greater. This is the argument underlying the 'too big to fail' hypothesis which addresses, in its more sophisticated form, the risk that the closure or 'winding-down' of a large and complex banking organisation will be disorderly and thus threaten economic stability.

In a similar manner, financial capital market concentration may be assessed by examining comparable stock and bond market concentration ratios.[18] Together with the financial market reliance ratio – the ratio of total non-bank liabilities to total liabilities as a measure of the economy's reliance on financial markets to finance economic activity – the financial market concentration ratios offer a snapshot of the relative economic importance of a nation's capital markets in financing overall economic activity.[19]

These aggregate indicators crudely capture sources of systemic fragility that are consistent with the structural–functional perspective of this study. The indicators derive, primarily, from the balance sheet for a nation, yet to explore the differences in crises across nations and over time require more specific disaggregated portfolio detail.

Who finances whom, how and for what? Disaggregating the balance sheet

The potential for systemic crises within the financial system itself is created by the extent to which the portfolio of one institution includes common collateral assets with, loans to or equity in, that of another financial institution. At least three related portfolio relationships operate to spread the initial distress. One channel operates indirectly through changes in the real value of debt outstanding whenever portfolios are linked indirectly by way of holding in common collateral assets. A second channel operates directly through changes in the unit cost of debt service wherever portfolios are linked directly through inter-institution lending and shared debt instruments.[20] In this second channel, the level of debt of a given firm affects the cost of servicing debt for other, otherwise unrelated, firms. A third channel may operate through changing equity values to the extent that the portfolio of one institution includes equity in that of another.

The aggregated balance sheet data discussed earlier offer a first approximation to the map of the financial structure and its relation to the underlying structure of the economy. Any consistent comparison of crises across different financial structures and stages of economic development demands, however, a clearer, more precise picture of who financed whom, how and for what. Related to this core question is the question of how and to what extent are financial portfolios in key sectors linked together? If the debt levels are rising, which enterprises or sectors are most exposed? To what extent is a speculative run up in the prices of assets driving an expansion of credit, increasing the debt to income ratios of speculators and lenders and increasing portfolio fragility by forcing an ever-greater reliance on capitals gains to service the rising debt? These and other such questions can only be addressed by examining more closely the constituent elements of the aggregated balance sheet.

The second approximation to a map of the financial structure would entail disaggregating by primary issuer and primary holder of the nation's stock of liabilities. Where the first approximation identifies total financial liabilities (assets), the second approximation would identify this information in terms of portfolios for the five key sectors of the economy – household, government, financial, non-financial and the foreign sectors. Institutional details for a given economy would inform the third approximation expansion. In systems wherein the liquidity of sector portfolios cannot be adjusted by access to deep asset markets, financial fragility is linked closely to the term structure of debt relative to the term structure of financial assets. Thus, differentiating the debt structure by distinguishing between short-term from longer-term maturities would provide useful information. For substantially open economies, with sectors issuing debt denominated in foreign currencies, disaggregating portfolios by currency denomination would expose the core information needed to determine the degree of risk derivative of currency fluctuations.

Consideration of the manner in which financial portfolios link spheres of production might usefully guide further refinements of the national balance sheet. Disaggregating the non-financial sector into agricultural, manufacturing and commercial sectors, for example, would illuminate the extent to which these broad production sectors are linked financially either directly through interlocking portfolios or indirectly through third party portfolios. Such refinement would permit as well an ability to locate more precisely the origin of the speculation and to identify more precisely the precipitating source of the credit expansion.[21]

In sum, once a financial event has become systemic,

> effects on the real economy are generally thought to occur potentially through three channels. First, payment system disruptions… may cause the failure of illiquid but solvent firms. Second, disruptions to credit flows may create severe reductions in the supply of funds to finance profitable investment opportunities in the non-financial sector. Third, collapses in asset prices… may induce failures of financial as well as non-financial firms and households, and decrease economic activity through a decline in wealth and an increase in uncertainty.
>
> (Group of Ten, 2001: 127)

The threat of a systemic financial crisis – as a crisis that causes extreme economic hardship on those otherwise unconnected with the institution or market initially disrupted – derives from the combination of the above factors. While the debt burden in a major sector or industry of the economy creates the core vulnerability, the potential for the distress to spread derives from the extent to which the economy is linked to this vulnerable sector by and through the financial system networks. In short, for a given vulnerability, systemic fragility is greater the more concentrated the financial system, the more concentrated the financial portfolios in shared liabilities and the more extensively integrated the financial system with commercial and investment activity.[22]

Evolving fragilities

While potentially extremely useful for facilitating comparative analyses of crises across episodes, the balance sheet framework could, were the data consistently available at higher frequencies, offer important insights into the evolution of a given speculation-crisis episode.[23] It is conjectured that these same systemic fragilities will amplify as an episode unfolds. As a given speculation bids up the price of financial assets related to the innovation and encourages an expansion of credit with an increased concentration supporting the speculation, the relative size of the financial sector will increase, the financial integration with speculative investment activity will increase and the portfolios and financial asset markets will become more concentrated in the speculative assets. As speculation extends and promotes financial integration, the risk increases that distress will spread on its eventual recession. Not only is there the systemically fragile nature of intrinsic linkages inherent in the operation of debt markets (of the type that Irving Fisher [1932, 1933] describes in his debt-deflation scenario), but this fragility increases as the speculation continues in the manner described by Hyman Minsky (1982a,b, 1986) and summarised in Chapter 6, feeding back into the fragility of the financial sector. As the fragility of the household and non-financial corporate portfolios increase with speculation, creditor institutions become more vulnerable. As the IMF (2001: 9) states,

> The key role played by corporate borrowers in recent episodes of financial sector distress demonstrates the importance of monitoring developments in this sector.... There is strong evidence that levels of corporate leverage, in particular, influence the ability of firms to withstand [shocks that affect future cash flow and value of collateral]. The more leveraged and the less liquid the corporate sector, the more vulnerable it is to shocks.

Thus, a financial accounts matrix showing both changes in financial assets and in liabilities, complemented by balance sheet information, 'would provide important statistical information on the decisions of economic agents to alter the level and composition of their financial portfolios' of assets and liabilities (Mink and Silva, 2003: 12).

Conjectural illustrations

Were we able to complete with some accuracy such a snapshot of the financial network periodically over time and across countries, we would have at our disposal a means of systematically tracking the evolution of crises. We would be able to identify the expansion of financial equity and debt arising out of the speculation; we could identify quantitatively the direct impact on financial portfolios once the speculative enthusiasm waned and trace the transmission paths of distress out to otherwise unrelated spheres of the economy. In this way, in a completed balance sheet for all sectors, networked exposures to markets versus institutional sources of debt-based fragility would become apparent, as would the taxonomic distinctions between public, corporate and private financing fragilities. Like so, we could render visible variations of crisis episodes within a country over time and across countries at a point in time.

For example, the consensus causes of the Southeast Asian crises in 1997 include the currency and liability mismatches in the portfolios of the deposit banks. Not only were the banks borrowing in foreign currency denominated, short-term debt, they were also lending in domestic currency for long term, illiquid infrastructure projects. The systemic nature of the crises derived, allegedly, from the relative importance of deposit banks in financing a relatively high proportion of domestic economic activity. If this is a reasonable explanation of the portfolio vulnerabilities and networked linkages, we would expect to see these aspects reflected in the balance sheet data. Specifically, we would expect to see a high proportion of Thai bank liabilities obtained from the rest of the world, denominated in foreign currencies, and due in the short-term financing longer term assets denominated in domestic currency as loans to Thai utilities and property companies. We would also expect to see both a high bank intermediation ratio and high concentration ratio, reflecting the national importance of indirect financing of a substantial portion of Thai production by the five large banks in this emerging economy.

In comparison, the crisis in 1720–1721 England was a crisis in public finance, with government finances linked critically and extensively to the East India Company through the London banks. The greater network of finance from the London banks out to the country banks existed but financed a much smaller proportion of the total economic activity of England at the time. Analysis of contemporaneous bankruptcies suggests there was limited adverse impact beyond the collapse in share prices of East India Company stock and the failure of its primary creditor, the Sword Blade Bank. The conjecture is that confinement of England's distress is due to the limited extent of England's financial networks at this time. The balance sheet, were we able to complete it, might thus reveal a substantial proportion of government debt and East India stock held by London banks, a much lower proportion of government debt and Company stock held by banks outside London, and little of England's wider agricultural production reliant on the London banks for funding. Were a comparison of balance sheets to become possible, we might expect to see a lower financial development ratio, a higher bank intermediation ratio, a greater concentration of bank assets and lower and fewer portfolio links to the rest of the English economy in 1720 than that which might reveal themselves in the Thai balance sheet in 1997.

As important and informative as this may be, more important is the fact that we might then successfully confront one of the most fundamental of challenges in crisis research – the problem of *ex post* theorising. Once we move outside abstract reduced-form models populated by simple quantitative relationships into the complex world of institutions, broad networks, and narratives replete with historical specificity as explanations of crises, we lose the ability to produce testable representations and thus have no ability to easily confirm or refute particular hypotheses.[24] As Douglas Wood states in his 1983 review of Kindleberger's and Jean-Pierre Laffargue's collected papers on financial crises

> Unless historical studies provide for easy cross-section and cross-period comparisons, establishing the validity of posited relationships becomes a major problem, not least because we are always presented with *ex post* evidence associated with a crisis, rather than *ex ante* evidence of perhaps dozens of situations in which similar preconditions existed but no crisis occurred.
>
> (1983: 686)

What the balance sheet approach offers is the means necessary to make consistent cross-section and cross-country comparisons that would afford the institutional researcher a means of addressing this fundamentally important methodological challenge.

11 Evolving financial crises

Reflections and projections

Historical episodes of crises share many similarities. Speculation in innovation via financial claims on an identifiable subgroup of the economy's assets precedes most crises. Debt supports the speculation and plays a prominent role in causing the distress that follows. A withdrawal of credit available to finance activity in the wider economy constrains that activity and causes distress to spread well beyond the industries that had been the focal point of the prior speculation, affecting people and activity standing outside of and apart from that speculation. The subsequent economic and social crisis is more severe when the precipitating financial crisis involves the collapse of deposit banks.

The act of speculating occurs as a normal part of the capitalist process of accumulation and innovation. In Schumpeterian fashion, it is the commercialisation of technical invention together with its promise of material gain that motivates speculation. Though always present in the capitalist system, there are times when the possibility of material enrichment especially captivates the imagination of the individual. In periods of social and economic transition, brought about by an innovation of some importance, the potential to gain materially from the advance appears, to the individual, particularly high.

What motivates an individual to speculate in assets associated with the innovation is the promise of material enrichment. Located in a culture that values material wealth both for its own sake and for the non-material social advantages material wealth confer, speculative gain promises the individual both augmented material wealth and enhanced social status derivative of that prosperity. As a culture, then, capitalism implies that investor motivations extend beyond the maximisation of wealth for consumption-utility purposes. Investors are more than individual, rational, consumers seeking to enhance their utility from the consumption of goods and services; they are social beings with a need for group acceptance. Status in the group confers both a sense of belonging and a sense of individual importance – a manifestation of Georg Simmel's (1957) 'dualistic nature'. The culture of capitalism values material wealth for the non-monetary social worth – such as intelligence, rationality and industry – this wealth confers. There are clear class stratifications defined by the unequal distribution of material wealth and an ingrained status consciousness informed by monetary values. There is, to use Simmel's language, a 'reverence for the possession of money'. Within capitalist practices and forms of organisation, the possibilities inherent in the contractual transfer of wealth and property rights in the early stages of capitalism create the potential for individual advancement. The belief that one can advance oneself if one is intelligent and works hard dominates. However remote the possibility, however much the notion of full democratic access to wealth continues to contradict reality, the widespread *belief* that material gain and its associated social advancement are possible drives the speculating individual.

An innovation's true potential to offer material advance is fundamentally uncertain and dependent, in part, on the collective assessment of that potential. Social influences on the individual assessment of potential advance, and the presence of institutions that define the particular means by which the individual can speculate in the innovation, create the potential for a destabilising speculation of the type that forewarns a crisis. Institutions and financial crises both owe their core existence to the presence of incalculable uncertainty of the type discussed by Frank Knight (1964 [1921]). Were all outcomes measurable and transaction costs negligible, we would observe neither institutions – as rules and conventions governing behaviour – failing nor extreme market dislocations brought on by massive speculation and panic in the adaptation to major innovations.

Innovations that induce growth in the capitalist system need not be limited to innovations in tangible capital. Innovations in financial institutions have facilitated growth by lowering individual transactions costs. Examples of innovations in financial products and services created to meet the needs of financing investment include bills of exchange to finance transnational trade, joint stocks to raise financial capital and insurance products to spread risk. Initial innovations in finance lowered transactions costs by offering a means to spread risk across individuals at a point in time. More recently, innovations in the form of derivative instruments offer a means for spreading risk across individuals across time.

As an experiment never before tried, we cannot predict the effect of the innovation; hence, we cannot predict the full range of potential outcomes. Without any objective future information on which to base anticipations of speculative advance, speculators default in using current information and devising simple rules to aid in its interpretation. Specifically, speculators observing the initial advances consider that the advances will continue. In seeking to comprehend the changing world, individuals rely on social meanings in and social understandings of the unfolding events. Observing that others share the same optimistic opinion reinforces the speculator, further encouraging the speculative optimism and resulting activity. In a roundabout manner, then, uncertainty with respect to the innovation's future material outcome opens the door to collective influence through the individual's reliance on the shared opinion of others. Where the speculative activity itself materially affects the innovation's potential, the material outcome becomes dependent on the collective assessment of the potential outcome. The key to understanding how the financial crisis can happen and how it unfolds, lies in understanding how behaviour is motivated when information is incomplete and imperfect in a shifting landscape, because it is in these periods of transition and advance that the potential for a collective dynamic to swamp the individual investment decision is, as a matter of degree, especially high and the financial system especially fragile.

Institutions exist to create order and predictability where uncertainty promises disorder and chaos. Institutions may be formal legal constructions grounded in capitalist notions of property rights or they may be informal codes of conduct patterning communitarian exchange. By patterning human interaction in a manner that renders the social at once predictable and defining, the individual is at once constrained by and freed in her or his actions.

The capitalist institutions that concern us here are those particular to finance. Finance capitalism is a form and dimension of capitalism characterised by the impersonal transfer of contracts, evidencing claims to wealth and defining the particular means by which the individual undertakes the speculation. In a system of finance capitalism, not only have the intrinsic values of tangible assets – such as factories and inventories – been externalised in the process of converting to money values, so too have the values of intangible assets or knowledge in the form of information, patents and trademarks. The formal financial institutions that characterise finance capitalism are those institutions that provide the means of transferring wealth and purchasing power from suppliers to users of funds. Formal financial institutions include the contractual claims on wealth, the markets in which these claims may be traded, and the legal entities, such as banks, whose primary business is defined – in both function and by a portfolio of assets – by the process of creating and transferring credit. The means to speculate in an innovation are provided for by the formal financial institutions that define finance capitalism.

Financial institutions, by offering the individual a means of lowering the perceived risk of loss from investment and speculation, encourage, in turn, innovations in non-financial capital. In the partitioning of an asset's value in the manner afforded by joint stocks, for example, funding innovation becomes easier. With only part ownership of an innovative asset, the required financial commitment of the individual speculator is lower. Where the claims to part ownership are tradable, the ability to extract that commitment becomes potentially easier. By creating an easier means by which to speculate in the tangible innovations, financial institutions have encouraged the speculative supply of funds available to support non-financial innovation and have thus promoted investment in the non-financial innovation itself.

Financial institutions can therefore be growth inducing. Recalling the role collective opinion plays in the assessment of speculative prospects and allowing for the increased ease with which financial institutions support the means to speculate, we are closer to seeing how, in an environment of uncertainty born of innovation, speculative enthusiasm of the type that foreshadows a crisis may appear. When the material outcome of the innovation is uncertain, collective influence in defining the anticipations of advance intrudes. Shared opinion of the potential for advance influences the degree of actual speculation and thus the extent to which funds are available to finance the innovation. If the extent to which the promise of an innovation may be realised is dependent on the available funding, the increased funding will ensure initial advance and further feed the speculative enthusiasm.

In all crises of historical note, the speculations preceding them were debt financed. Credit, in the manner analysed by Minsky, Schumpeter and Keynes, amplifies the swings inherent in the underlying real capitalist economy. The possibility of borrowing to speculate further encourages speculative activity by providing both the means for easier participation and a greater motivation. Borrowing a portion of the value of contractual claim on wealth reduces the initial outlay required, further lowers the financial commitment of the speculator, and increases the ease with which individuals may speculate. Initially motivated by the potential for material gain, individuals acquiring financial assets on margin will face the prospect of an even greater gain. As is widely understood, the lower the equity stake in an asset, the greater the individual's net gain from a given increase in the value of the asset. As is widely understood, too, the converse holds and the greater the financial leverage, the greater the financial distress from a given decrease in the value of the asset. When a financial crisis involves the collapse of a deposit bank, the payments system that supports day-to-day commercial activity is lost, and the collapse shatters the certainty derived from the symbolic importance of banks as a stable institution in the capitalist system.

While elements of the above exist in all financial crises of historical note, the particulars of each crisis vary considerably in a host of institutional detail. The specific details of each crisis depend on the existing financial structure or matrix of financial instruments and institutions that constitute a nation's financial system at that specific point in history. The focus of the prior speculation and subsequent collapse depend on both the particular innovation and the types of financial contracts available to finance speculative activity. How the contraction of credit affects all other industries depends on the extent to which these other industries rely on the same markets or lending institutions for the supply of credit. Thus, the manner in which the crisis spreads from the centre out to peripheral economic activities depends on the particular network of credit linkages.

A few preliminary theses arise out of this study. First, the more revolutionary the innovation, the greater is the potential for a speculative enthusiasm to become widespread among the population. Where the ultimate potential for an innovation is dependent on the extent to which it is adopted to create new activities and adapted to mould existing ones, the enthusiasm for speculation will feedback to influence the innovation's potential. Second, the more accessible the means by which one may speculate, the greater will be the intensity of the speculation in a given revolutionary innovation. As stock markets are the principal means for promoting speculation in revolutionary innovations, this hypothesis would often translate empirically into accessibility of stock markets; where market accessibility is encouraged by a variety of institutional factors including the institutional freedom of non-professionals to bypass the professionals, the liquidity of the market and the speculator's access to credit. Third, the manner in which credit may either be extended to support and promote the prior speculation or contracted so as to facilitate the transmission of the distress depends critically on the level of development of the financial structure and the nature of the particular financial instruments and enterprises that comprise that structure. Fourth, the longer the process of diffusing the revolutionary innovation, the more fragile the environment becomes. Over time, as a speculative enthusiasm gains in popularity and intensity, supported and promoted by an accumulation of debt, the ability of both people and the financial system to adjust to a slowdown declines.

In purely economic terms, the ability of speculators to service the accumulating debt depends increasingly on sustained capital gains. While a levelling off of prices early in an episode of speculation may cause hardship for a few, if the speculation continues, an increasing number of indebted speculators will experience financial distress in the eventual slowdown. This financial fragility will be coupled with a fragility stemming from the increasing rigidity of confidence in the current state of affairs. With no other basis but past history on which to form expectations of the future, the longer the history, the more secure people become in believing that recent past experience defines the present. With greater confidence comes greater risk that a material change in circumstance will shatter the certainty. Finally, the more tightly and broadly linked is the economy through social and financial networks, the greater is the potential for either the prior enthusiasm or the subsequent distress or both to spread to other sectors in the economy. This potential for contagion determines whether the distress stays localised and contained or becomes systemic thereby threatening the stability of the wider economy. Conversely, looser and more limited integration – either intrinsically as was the case in 1720 England or instrumentally as a result of lender-of-last-resort policy actions by monetary authorities – will limit the 'systemic risk' of a crisis.

To fully characterise the financial structure will entail a combination of quantitative and qualitative indicators that are capable of representing such variety with enough flexibility so as to accommodate the remarkable assortment of contemporary and historical financial instruments, processes and enterprises. While such a comprehensive description thus far escapes us, exploring the extent to which a rudimentary balance sheet framework could illuminate the structure and our understanding of the historical differences in crises. Such a preliminary exploration of the basic hypothesis could be undertaken in a manner that encompasses a variety of seemingly disparate research on financial fragility.

As speculation continues, the increase in debt-to-equity ratios and the like reflects an increasing vulnerability of the overall system. Endogenously, therefore, speculation creates its own fragility. This endogenous fragility implies that an economy in the early stages of a speculation may be able to withstand a shock of a given magnitude, but that same shock could eventually fracture the system. The crisis is then not in terms of excess speculation. Neither is it necessarily or strictly in terms of Ponzi financing. Instead, the crisis is simply – but importantly – the inability of the capitalist system to periodically withstand shocks. The speculative inclinations of investors and the ability of the financial system to accommodate and support the speculation with credit creation are both common features of capitalism. Crises, in other words, are the outcome of precisely the same behaviour that capitalism rewards and encourages and by which we define the culture of capitalism.

The characteristics of the crisis will vary, however, depending on the stage of economic and financial development. A financial market collapse that hits an economy in the early stages of development will be less severe than one that hits the financial institutions if the functional importance of the market for the economy is relatively small. Contrariwise, a crisis that hits the banking system in an economy in the early stages of development – where the banking system provides the primary media of exchange and funds for commercial activity – will be devastating. In advanced economies, with well-developed financial markets providing an alternative mechanism for the management of liquidity and transfer of funds to finance commercial and investment activity, the potential for a market collapse that interferes with the economy's allocation mechanisms becomes greater. Finally, over time as the financial system becomes more integrated with the economy and the economy becomes more interconnected through and by the linkages afforded by the financial networks, we might expect the threat of crises to become more general and widespread and less specific or concentrated in a given area of economic activity in the absence of containment policies such as last-resort lending.

Although the institutions of finance capitalism exist generally to reduce uncertainty and do so insofar as they structure in a predictable manner the means by which the system creates and transfers credit, these same institutions permit ignorance by replacing the incentives to gain the lost information with the conditions that support a belief that to avoid the information is costless. By partitioning wealth into contractual claims on the underlying assets of the economy, the institutions separate the owner of capital from the manager of capital, in some cases by a good distance. The loss of important qualitative information about the management operations and the like could be recouped by the owners of capital were they so inclined, but the costs of doing so outweigh the costs of simply extracting oneself if the promise of advance fails to be realised. From the perspective of the individual, ignoring the business specific, qualitative information is efficient despite the ignorance being inefficient for the economy as a whole. By introducing deposit banks, some of the sources of qualitative information could be accessed, but the traditional maturity mismatch in bank portfolios combined with the unique characteristics of the bank's liabilities means that the financial system becomes that much more dependent on the state of confidence.

Herein we have both the source of the crisis and the contradictions of finance capitalism as a cumulative causation, path-dependent process. How the crisis unfolds depends on pre-existing financial structure and the crises themselves are transformative in that they have the potential to generate changes to that structure. Moreover, speculation and subsequent crises have the potential to alter the investment generally and investment in innovation specifically. Path dependence – in the sense that where we are limits the choices over where we might go – is thus a critical element of the framework. Where the institutions of finance capitalism provide the means to encourage speculation and thus drive the innovation and accumulation that define the capitalist system, these same institutions contain the seeds of crises. The potential to leverage one's speculative investment in an innovation at once encourages that speculation and ensures the increasing fragility of the process. Where the institutions of finance capitalism exist to reduce uncertainty and thus promote stability, they do so by creating a means of speculating that supports a wilful ignorance of available information, thus creating uncertainty and introducing a threat of instability where none previously existed. In periods when speculative activity ebbs and the economy declines, the possibility that individual decisions to extract themselves from the speculative assets swamps the ability of the institutions to process the requests, the action results in the collective inability to sell and in higher costs to the individual. What is true for the individual and beneficial in the advance does not hold true for the economy in periods of decline. Thus, the institutions of finance capitalism reduce uncertainty by creating what can be, at times, only the illusion of certainty.

Notes

1 An introduction to the evolution of financial fragility

1 In the contemporary debates, the differences in interpretation appear as points of disagreement. De Long (1999: 257) summarises these points of disagreement as questions: 'Are flexible exchange rates a help or hindrance? Is IMF support [as a lender of last resort] in a crisis a cure or a cause? And does recovery and a resumption of capital flows require deep-rooted financial sector reforms to diminish corruption and improve transparency and corporate governance?' Based on his analysis of crises prior to the First World War, De Long suggests the answer is no to the latter two questions and supports adopting a form of fixed exchange rates to reintroduce stability.

2 Hoppit (1986) and Davis (2002) offer, separately and for different periods in history, possible taxonomies of financial crises. Hoppit's distinction between the public, private and corporate crises in eighteenth-century England appears to have little in common, however, with Davis' theory-based distinctions between late twentieth-century crises. Kindleberger (1989) labels financial crisis a 'hardy perennial' and offers important insight into elements critical to a study of crises informed by Minsky's (1986) valuable Financial Instability Hypothesis. Kindleberger's historical lists of speculative objects and focal points of distress appear, however, somewhat random, and Minsky himself limited his analysis to the mid-twentieth-century American economy.

3 The term 'finance capital' is borrowed from Hilferding, (1981 [1910]: 225) to mean a state wherein 'an ever-increasing proportion of the capital used in industry is finance capital, capital at the disposition of the banks which is used by the industrialists'.

4 The perspective adopted in this study fits within the 'institutionalist approach' as defined by Hodgson (1998) and Samuels (1995), where the concern is primarily about the distribution of power 'with markets as institutional complexes operating within and in interaction with other institutional complexes; with causes and consequences of individual and collective psychology; with the formation of knowledge, or what is taken as knowledge, in a world of radical indeterminacy about the future' (Samuels, 1995: 571).

5 These three chapters expand and elaborate on the thesis presented in Visano (2004).

2 Illustrations of manias, panics and crises

1 The South Sea Company was initially created in May of 1711 to buy up the short-term debt of the government.

> The primary motivation for the company from the beginning was to fund a major part of the total national debt, accepting a lower interest on its share of the national debt than had been paid by the government previously. This interest received from the government, plus an annual management fee, provided the cash flow for dividend payments to shareholders, whose shares were more easily transferable than the short-term debt they had replaced.
>
> (Neal, 1990: 52)

2

> Only one-tenth to one-fifth of the sale price was paid at the time of subscription, and the remaining payments were stretched up to three years... But because the total sold on margin at that time amounted to only slightly over 10% of the total capital that would be in existence at the end of the debt conversion, it does not seem plausible that the money subscriptions were the primary contrivance used to blow up the bubble. They were the main device for speculators, but not the primary cause of the bubble itself.
>
> (Neal, 1990: 100–101)

3 The historical details reveal some important nuances. Price increases were clearly demand driven in the spring of 1720. Transfer books were closed on 23 June 1720 and subsequent price increases, according to Neal (1990: 104), were due to a decrease in the supply of credit that caused the forward premium on shares to rise in anticipation of the reopening of the transfer books on 22 August 1720.

4 These values are as cited in Davies (1994) and differ slightly from those values quoted in Garber (1990). The values are only estimates, given the complexity of the terms of the conversion. Moreover, quotations may or may not include dividends, see Neal (1990: 101). For the purpose here, sorting out and explaining the difference in estimates is immaterial. For a clear analysis of the influence of the French experience under John Law's system on the English experience through international capital flows, see Neal (1990: Ch 4).

5 Over the thirty years prior to June of 1720, it had become customary to permit the existence of unauthorised joint-stock companies. The 'Bubble Act' – principally an act to create two new insurance companies – included as an add-on, a clause that prohibited the operation of companies that did not have a charter detailing a specified and definite purpose. The ban was apparently the result of a campaign led by the directors of the South Sea Company concerned that the rising competition for 'investable' funds would constrain funds available for their company's stock.

6 Schubert (1988: 303) addresses the international dimension of the financial panic as the stress in London caused the capital held by Dutch and French investors to flee to safety in the Bank of Amsterdam. Ashton (1959), quoting George Chalmers, supports the claim that it was public credit that was chiefly affected.

7 This view is shared by many, including Tooke (1838) and Andréadès (1966).

8 The precise event that sparks the panic is an open question. Jenks (1927) names the January 1826 suspension of debt payments by Columbia. Pressnel (1956: 485) names the quarterly contraction imposed on bankers by the need to pay monies to the government, despite the fact that the Bank of England would pay out an equivalent sum in quarterly dividends soon afterwards.

9 Hughes (1956) in an analysis of the 1857 commercial crisis states, however, that there had been no 'excessive speculation' in 1847.
10 The 'crisis of 1847', hitting its worst in October of that year, was a crisis in credit – ocurring when the failure of corn dealers in London and Liverpool in August of 1847 weakened the lending houses 'and like a house of cards, the over-strained credit structure collapsed' (Ward-Perkins, 1950: 78) – and a crisis in cotton. The latter was due to abnormally low cotton production and a recoil from a cotton boom that may be 'partially explained by over-assessment of the new China market and cotton exports' (Ward-Perkins, 1950: 88).
11 The origins of the European banking crisis precipitated locally by the collapse of the Creditanstalt can be traced back to the decrease in the net American long-term foreign lending (see Fleisig, 1975).
12 De Long (1999), citing Goldstein (1998) and Radelet and Sachs (1998), suggests that it was a shift in foreign investor opinion about the relative proportion of Asian investments that caused the reversal. 'Yet once investors in New York and elsewhere had decided that they had invested too large a share of their portfolios in Asia, the rapid shift in opinion and in capital flows had the same consequences as in Mexico [in 1994] and western Europe [in 1992] previously.' Richard Cooper (1999: 283) in his comments on De Long argues that the 1997 Asian financial crisis 'reflected the mismatch between the requirements of their real economies and the evolution of their financial systems'.

3 Capitalism: a culture of accumulation as the context for innovation

1 That some wealthy individuals may not be of high moral fibre causes outrage when society learns of the fraud. The possibility that the wealthy may engage in deception confronts and contradicts an accepted understanding that to be wealthy is to be morally superior. Wealthy individuals deemed guilty of fraud are outliers, exceptions to the norm. Considering that their fraudulent behaviour is wholly consistent with notions of competition promoted by capitalism is beyond the realm of possibilities.
2 The use of the term 'primary process' is intentionally used as an allusion to Joseph Schumpter's primary business cycle. The interested reader is referred to Schumpeter's (1939) *Business Cycles* for a detailed treatment of the manner in which innovation spawns the ebb and flow of business activity of the type that explains the primary cycle.
3 Economic historians of technology label differently similar distinctions. Freeman *et al.* (1982: 83) for example, work with 'radical' as distinct from 'major' innovation. The former 'may give rise to a change in technique in one or more branches of industry, or may themselves give rise to one or more new branches of industry', whereas the latter gives rise to 'new products and new processes in existing branches of industry'.
4 Earlier revolutionary inventions in information communication technologies lie at the heart of many recent economic developments. The rise in relative importance of a parallel electronic economy and the restructuring of the business services and financial services industries are examples.
5 For the study of financial manias and panics – as extreme episodes of financial instability exhibiting clear evidence of a collective or social dynamic – it is important to differentiate conceptually between the economic and social impacts of the innovation. This issue will be explored in a later work. For now, it is

sufficient to note that the distinction offered earlier between a potential revolutionary impact and the necessity of social change in realising that potential is a finer distinction than that offered by Rosenberg and other writers of the economic history of technology.

6 According to these process and impact criteria, railroads, motorcars, radios and television, and the universal computer are all examples of revolutionary innovations. The exercise of running down a complete historical list of innovations with an eye to labelling each innovation as either evolutionary or revolutionary will, however, frustrate and disappoint. Such a blunt dichotomy will fail us as a precise instrument by which we may categorise each and every historical innovation. The reader is therefore cautioned that, while such stark contrasts will serve us well in developing the basic ideas of our theory of financial instability, in reality these two categories of innovation are conceived of best as defining the bounds of a spectrum along which any given innovation lies. Rather than defining two mutually exclusive, all-encompassing categories, a given innovation may in reality be more evolutionary in nature than revolutionary but may contain elements of the latter, for example; and vice versa.

7 This view fits broadly with Schumpeter's view of technological leading sectors as an (imperfect) explanation for Kondratieff's (1935) long waves and Simon Kuznets' (1930) notion that 'primary trends in production and prices reflected systematically the life cycle of a given technical innovation (or opening up of a new territory or natural resource)' (as quoted in Rostow, 1975: 721). With competition, the introduction of an innovation can destabilize if and when the rush to imitate the leaders results in adoption rates that nearer maturity prove to be excessive (see Perelman, 1999).

4 The impact of uncertainty on (in)forming behaviour

1 '...professional investment may be likened to those newspaper competitions in which the competitors have to pick out the six prettiest faces from a hundred photographs, the prize being awarded to the competitor whose choice most nearly corresponds to the average preferences of the competitors as a whole; so that each competitor has to pick, not those faces which he himself finds prettiest, but those which he thinks likeliest to catch the fancy of the other competitors, all of whom are looking at the problem from the same point of view. It is not a case of choosing those which, to the best of one's judgement, are really the prettiest, nor even those which average opinion genuinely thinks the prettiest. We have reached the third degree where we devote our intelligences to anticipating what average opinion expects the average opinion to be. And there are some, I believe, who practise the fourth, fifth and higher degrees'. Keynes (1973a [1936]: 156).

2 For a critique of the significant but one-sided contribution of the French Conventions School, see Bibow, Lewis, and Runde (2005).

3 In a model with heterogeneous investors differentiated by a non-homogeneous distribution of perceptual abilities, Kaen and Rosenman (1986) argue that the peak volume of trading corresponds to the mode of the perceptual distribution.

4 The distinction between 'leaders' and 'followers' becomes blurred if, as De Long *et al.* (1990) suggest, leaders anticipate the actions of followers and act in anticipation of the effect of the actions of followers. Suggested by the investment strategy of Soros (1987), De Long *et al.* (1990: 380) model positive feedback trading wherein rational speculators bet not on future fundamentals but on

future crowd behaviour, 'buying in anticipation of further buying by uninformed investors'.

5 Conventional approaches: speculation as a fool's paradise

1 See Burmeister (1980), for example, for an accessible treatment of the capital-theoretic problem.
2 Subsequent work qualified these conclusions. Tax implications of adjusting a firm's debt-to-equity ratio (Modigliani and Miller, 1963; Stiglitz, 1973), bankruptcy costs (Stiglitz, 1972) and imperfect information leading to credit rationing (Stiglitz and Weiss, 1981) could each generate results whereby the financial structure of the firm does matter.
3 In different vocabulary, I refer here to the situation in which the innovation drives up the natural rate of interest above the market rate of interest set by lending institutions, such that the anticipated returns from undertaking the endeavour outweighs the cost of borrowing the funds to do so. Variations in the term structure of lending rates over the course of the business cycle – with greatest variation experienced in the shorter-term maturities – are a key element of Minsky's (1986) Financial Fragility Hypothesis. This is, in essence, Wicksell's cumulative process, insofar as Wicksell's use of the 'natural' rate interest is consistent with a marginal product of capital (see Laidler, 1999, 2003a).
4 The addition of naïve speculators imitating professionals with access to credit creates an instability that was essentially John Stuart Mill's (1965[1848]: BkIII Ch XII para III.12.11) explanation of the commercial crisis of 1825.

> The most usual cause of [commercial crises] is the recoil of process after they have been raised in the spirit of speculation, intense in degree, and extending to many commodities. Some accident which excites the speculation of rising prices, such as the opening of a new foreign market,...sets speculation at work in several leading department at once. The prices rise, and the holders realize, or appear to have the power of realizing, great gains. In certain states of the public mind, such examples of rapid increase of fortune call forth numerous imitators and speculation goes much beyond what is justified by the original grounds for expecting rise of price, but extends itself to articles in which there never was any such ground...At periods of this kind a great extension of credit takes place. Not only do all whom the contagion reaches employ their credit much more freely than usual; but they really have more credit, because they seem to be making unusual gains, and because a generally reckless and adventurous feeling prevails, which disposes people to give as well as take credit more largely than at other times, and give it to persons not entitled to it. In this manner, in the celebrated speculative year 1825...the prices of many of the principal articles of commerce rose greatly, without any fall in others.... When, after such a rise, the reaction comes, and prices begin to fall, though at first perhaps only through the desire of the holders to realize, speculative purchases cease: but were this all, process would only fall to the level from which they rose, or to that which is justified by the state of the consumption and of the supply. They fall, however, much lower; for as, when prices are rising, and everybody apparently making a fortune, it was easy to obtain almost any amount of credit, so now, when everybody seems to be losing, and many fail entirely, it is with difficulty that firms of known solidity can obtain even the credit to which they are accustomed, and which it is the greatest inconvenience

> to be without; because all dealers have engagements to fulfil, and nobody feeling sure that the portion of his means which he is entrusted to others will be available in time, no one likes to part with ready money, or to postpone his claim to it. To these rational considerations there is superadded, in extreme cases, a panic unreasoning as the previous overconfidence; money is borrowed for short periods at almost any rate of interest, and sales of goods for immediate payment are made at any sacrifice. Thus general prices, during a commercial revulsion, fall as much below the usual level as during the previous period of speculation they have risen above it: the fall, as well as the rise, originating not in anything affecting money, but in the state of credit. . . .

Such a view is later echoed by Alfred Marshall (1923), among others.

6 Justifications and means: the institutional organisation of speculation

1 Where education credentials and performance indicators attempt to quantify what are essentially qualitative products, we risk exclusive focus on the quantitative, losing an appreciation for the value of qualitative, as the majority respond to the biased incentives. Where qualitative judgments are subjective, confidence becomes an integral factor in the judgement of quality and thus assessment of any success. In the case of monetary policy, for example, where the consumer inflation rate is the primary performance indicator but where clear channels of central bank influence are unknown, the focus of policy announcements focuses on convincing the public of central bank influence, see Spotton and Rowley (1996); and Pigeon (2004); Rowley and Visano (2004).

2 To the extent that some of the valuable information remains available – if only more difficult to obtain – investors would only seek out that information if the costs of obtaining it were less than the individual's perceived costs of ignoring it under the assumption that investors are maximising expected net returns. As we shall see shortly, however, the individual's perceived costs of ignoring it are smaller the more liquid the asset. Of course, what holds true for the individual cannot hold true in the aggregate.

3 Related to this problem of a dilution of the control over capital is a free rider problem, as identified by Berle and Means (1932) and summarised in De Long (1999: 270): '[W]ho will monitor a firm's managers when shareholders have every incentive to free-ride on others' monitoring of those managers?'

4 The history of economic development attributes the impulse to change as one stemming from physical changes that affect the manufacturing process – it may be the discovery of a new market for inputs or outputs or a new product that in turn creates new markets and alters the vector of relative prices. The history of technical invention – as the source of a new product – tends to focus on the economy of energy, interpreting technical change as one motivated and promoted by the continual search for more efficient and cheaper sources of power in the most limited, physical sense. What is proposed here is the broadening of the definition of innovation to include institutional innovations – such as the introduction of the joint-stock company – that occur in the absence of any physical invention but nevertheless prove revolutionary in impact.

5 Rostow (1975) relies on this critical aspect of innovation to explore the consistent, but imperfect, secular trend theories of Kondratieff (1935), Schumpeter (1939) and Kuznets (1930) and to promote his own 'leading sector' view.

6 Peter Bernstein (1998a) argues that an efficient market 'is a market without liquidity'. Davidson (1991: 138) writes,

> Successful entrepreneurs feeling the animal urge to action in the face of uncertainty will not make any significant decisions involving real resource commitments until they are sure of their liquidity position, so that they can meet their contractual (transaction demand) cash outlays over time.

7 Alchian (1950) derives this conclusion from a framework that allows for 'uncertainty' in the sense of an existence of a distribution of potential outcomes in combination with elements of luck.

8 Hong *et al.* (2004: 139) model stock market participation and social interaction, where the social investor 'finds it more attractive to invest in the market... when the participation among his peers is higher'. The channels through which interaction influences participation include word-of-mouth learning of the type Kelly and Grada (2000) identify as a possible explanation for the neighbourhood effect in their study of the 1854 and 1857 bank panics.

9 'For the London Stock Exchange, the earliest printed evidence of price quotations of which we are aware comes from a weekly price list: Whiston's *The Merchant Remembrancer*, for 4 July 1681.' The date is not likely to be pushed back much further in the British Press. The Printing Act of 1663 had eliminated all newspapers in England, except for the *London Gazette*. When that act... lapsed in 1679, a number of newspapers arose 'to exploit the passions of the dreaded London mob', (Neal, 1990: 21; with quote from Cope, 1978: 5).

10 The distinction between the professional and naïve speculator, while useful for the present purpose, is a bit too crude. In the initial stages of an episode, those contemplating speculation for the first time are reasonably considered, by definition, 'naïve'. As the speculation progresses, it is possible that some of these first-time speculators become interested enough in the financial system to undertake the education and training necessary to later assume the role of the professional speculator. So long as there remains some heterogeneity in speculators across knowledge and understanding of the financial process – that is, some differentiation along the lines of Heiner's decision-competence gap – the material elements of the story apply.

7 The other side of the coin: the influence of credit creation and banks on speculation

1 Hawtrey (1965 [1879]) was convinced that the speculation of the 1920s was not sparked by a prior inflation, thus discrediting one important feature of the traditional monetary theory of the cycle (see Laidler, 2003a: 6). Borio and White (2004) cite recent evidence by Borio and Lowe (2002) where growth in asset prices and credit contain useful information about systemic banking distress. These interpretations sit in direct opposition to strict monetarist explanations of the cause of the credit cycle. Schwartz (1988) and Bordo and Wheelock (1998), for example, argue that sustained inflations encourage speculation and borrowing and that conversely, that 'monetary policy that focuses on limiting fluctuations in the price level will tend also to promote financial stability' (Bordo and Wheelock, 1998: 60).

2 This notion of a disparity between market rates of interest and the expected returns on a speculative endeavour is consistent with Robertson (1949 [1926]; 1928) who points out that 'inappropriate fluctuations in output were usually the result of market interest rates failing to catch up with the effects of innovation on the expected returns to investment' (quoted in Laidler (2003a: 17), which is compatible with Wicksell's idea of the cumulative process.

3 Minsky's explanation of the inherent instability of the capitalist system relies more on a credit cycle than I am proposing in this study. Where Minsky's instability can arise in the absence of any innovation, I place substantially more emphasis on the importance of innovation. The two perspectives are, however, compatible as they both assume fundamentally the presence of true uncertainty and the institutional importance of the financial system.

4 Inside money is any liability, such as a deposit liability, that operates as a medium of exchange. As both an asset and a liability of someone 'inside' the economy, the net liabilities for the economy equal zero. Outside money exists in net positive amounts for the economy.

8 Recoil in crisis: from peak to panic

1 Through portfolio effects, these three characteristics of crises may be dependent on one another. A sudden collapse of financial market prices may depress asset values to the point of extinguishing net worth, which in the case of a bank is primarily comprised of 'bank capital'. Similarly, if illiquidity forces a sale of assets in depressed markets, the effect on solvency will be the same.

2 Calomiris and Schweikart (1991) attribute the turning point from optimism to pessimism in the weeks preceding the American panic in 1857 to a change in expectations about the profitability of westward railroad expansion. Why this was so was not because of the effect of the end of the Crimean War on commodity prices, but rather because of a political struggle between 'free soil' and slavery in the territories that 'reduced the territories' attractiveness to new immigrants…and reduced the probability of the establishment of further settlements west of the territories, or of government involvement in a transcontinental railroad through Kansas' (1991: 816). This at a time when interest rates were rising.

3 Specifically, that the fruition of a major technological innovation reversed pressure on prices and, together with rising credit costs, narrowed profit margins.

4 'Just as soon as the lower classes begin to copy their style, thereby crossing the line of demarcation the upper classes have drawn and destroying the uniformity of their coherence, the upper classes turn away from this style…' (Simmel, 1957: 54).

5 Lang and Lang (1962: 342) characterise collective behaviour by spontaneity (governed primarily by mood), transitoriness (interaction results in impermanent forms) and volatility (derivative of a lack of orientation).

9 Societies in transition: time–space comparisons of financial instability

1

> For preindustrial economies and those in the early stages of industrialization…individuals may be unaccustomed to holding financial assets and unwilling to make use of financial intermediaries. Under such conditions, financial innovation – in the broadest sense, the introduction and utilization of new financial techniques and institutions – may assume an importance commensurate with technical innovations in industry.
>
> (Cameron and Patrick, 1967: 8)

2 For a detailed description of the bill of exchange as a means of payment and as a means of credit see Neal (1994: 157–162). Causality can and has run in the both directions; with new instruments introduced, their benefits can extend beyond the original purpose to drive further evolution and innovation in finance. The early twelfth century tally issued by the Exchequer of Receipt, for example,

was a notched wooden stick created as evidence of payment of taxes to the King of England. The tally stock, as the Exchequer's record of debt owed to the king, was assignable and soon employed by the king as an alternative means of Royal payment. Not only did the circulation of tallies permit the expansion of the money supply beyond the limits of minting, tallies evolved into a means of circumventing usury laws. As Davies states:

> At a time when usury was strictly forbidden and subject to the direst of penalties the tally became not only one of the main vehicles for circumventing prohibition, but a method of raising loans and extending credit, of acting as a wooden bill of exchange, and a sort of dividend coupon for royal debt.
>
> (Davies, 1994: 149)

Cameron (1967b: 317) attributes the popularity of bills of exchange as the 'favored instrument of credit' to the fact that usury laws effectively hindered the use of promissory notes.

3 Investment capital, at this time, was financed by a net supply of working capital (internal earnings), debt or attracting additional investors as partners or through the sale of joint stock. Apparently, 'the cost of equity for most firms was considered to be higher than the cost of debt for the entirety of the eighteenth century' (Neal 1994: 155).

4 This statement warrants an important qualification. As stated, it appears I would support the notion that historical evolution is linear – a continuous plan made up of periods and great events. In a strict Rostovian characterisation, it should be possible to fit a variety of national experiences into a single set of stages that runs linearly from take off, through a drive to maturity, into a stage of high mass consumption. While I employ reference to transitions across these stages to illustrate the importance of transitions in creating the environment prone to financial instability in the earlier discussion of episodes, as a theory of growth I am predisposed more to Gerschenkron's (1962) theory of relative backwardness which 'takes into account the specific initial conditions of a country'; see Rosovsky (1965). Further, there is a need to permit a role of agency and action critical in the performance of institutions; see Pollack (1998), for example. Thus the simpler reference to Rostow's stages is employed as a means of taxonomy only, not as a compatible theory of historical dynamics.

5 E.P. Thompson (1963), in his influential book on the making of the working class, raises questions around the whole nature of society and industrialisation under capitalist conditions and how changes interact to produce a cumulative effect (see Cohen, 1978: 53).

6 The concept of a joint-stock company with paid in capital ceded permanently to it by subscribers appears in 1650. '...the English East India Company did not make its capital permanent until the reorganization under Cromwell in 1650' (Neal 1990: 45).

7 For a description of the early intermediating financial functions provided by these groups, see Neal (1994: 165–168).

8 This is Davenant's estimate of the total money supply in England and Wales, as quoted in Davies (1994: 279).

9 While I retain the convention of referring to the 1720 English episode as a 'bubble', the reader might, by now, appreciate that I would want to significantly qualify its meaning here.

10 This Bubble Act, together with the memories of the losses of 1720, prevented the recurrence of any major stock boom in the eighteenth century.

> It did not, however, put an end to sudden expansions and contractions of credit: all that happened was that henceforth these manifested themselves less in the creation of new corporate enterprises than in speculation in the stock of existing companies and in commodities.
>
> (Ashton, 1959: 121)

Yet, institutional changes were not limited to the financial structure. Jones (1993) attributes the concept of the loyal opposition in the House of Lords as a legacy of the political reaction to the extensive corruption exposed by the bursting of the South Sea Bubble. See also, Neal (1998).

11 Post-crisis analysis debated the cause and effect, to which the credit expansion fuelled the speculative mania or the speculation in mining shares caused the credit expansion. The popular explanation (and politically expedient one for London bankers) lays blame on credit expansion from an excessive issue of country bank notes. The improbability of this as the sole or even primary causal impetus lies in the relatively small proportion of total credit that country bank notes comprised. Country bank issues never amounted to one-tenth part of the country's media of exchange, that total itself a small portion of total trade credit. (See Pressnel, 1956; Gilbart, 1968 [1882].

12 The suggestion that a crisis of liquidity precipitated the 1930s banking crisis is widely accepted. The suggestion that the stock market crash precipitated the liquidity crisis is more controversial. See Benston (1996) and White (1986).

13 As estimated in the *Survey of Consumer Finances*, this participation was both direct and indirect through mutual funds and various retirement vehicles. Just three years earlier, participation was 40.4 per cent. See Hong *et al.* (2004).

14 The following analysis relies heavily on Phongpaichit and Baker (2000).

15 Paralleling the withdrawal of funds from and spread of financial distress to countries perceived to be similarly fragile is the redirection of financial flows to economies perceived as safer havens. The rebalancing of portfolios in the wake of the Asian crisis saw a flight of capital from Asia into Europe and the United States. Van Wincoop and Yi (2000) attempt to trace the flow of capital out of Asia and find that a substantial part of it eventually reached the United States. The route by which Asian capital outflows become American financial inflows is indirect, first flowing into the offshore banking centers of Hong Kong, Cayman Islands and Singapore, among others, to European banks. The avenues by which funds flow from Europe to the United States are less clear save for the fact that they by-passed the American banking system. Whether or not these funds eventually found their way into the hi-tech stocks trading on the NASDAQ – thus feeding the recent hi-tech stock market bubble – is logically possible but as yet uncharted. Emmons and Schmid (2000) present evidence on large US firms to suggest that the Asian crisis resulted in increased stock market volatility in the United States and around the world. They also suggest that a shift in portfolio investments from Asia to the United States may explain why, despite increased uncertainty, increased stock market volatility, and falling after-tax earnings per share, the cumulative total return (dividends plus price change) for 1997–1998 on the S&P 100 index surged upward to more than 70 per cent (Visano 2004).

16 De Long (1999: 270) states:

> [T]he financial systems of East Asia – information asymmetries, tilted playing fields, and all – have supported the fastest growth over an entire generation that the world economy has seen anytime, anywhere. A decade ago their systems of financial organization were seen not as examples of

> destructive 'crony capitalism' but as adaptations of the Germano-Japanese system of large-scale bank-led finance that was efficient for late industrializers, at least until they caught up to the world's industrial leaders.

He cites (1999, 270 and 39) conversations with Barry Eichengreen and Jeffrey Frankel stressing the possibility that this system of financial organisation 'has advantages at the early stages and the Anglo-American system at later stages of development'.

17

> For preindustrial economies and those in the early stages of industrialization…[i]ndividuals may be unaccustomed to holding financial assets and unwilling to make use of financial intermediaries. Under such conditions, financial innovation – in the broadest sense, the introduction and utilization of new financial techniques and institutions – may assume an importance commensurate with technological innovation in industry.
>
> (Cameron and Patrick, 1967: 8)

18 Cameron and Patrick (1967: 6) for example, argue that of the formal financial system, the banking system is the 'most important' component. While true for the period of development and countries with which their comparative history is concerned, it may not hold true in the future, strictly speaking. Functionally, the manner in which banks can expand and contract credit so as to constitute a 'growth-inducing' factor of production (rather than merely acting as a passive facilitating agent) is not restricted to banks necessarily. We may see in the not-so-distant future, as information and communications technologies develop, the possibility of the traditional functions of the 'bank' – which are of critical importance – moving outside of the legal enterprises recognised as such.

19 'To prevent this volatility due to private sector bandwagon actions, what is required is a market-maker institution with sufficient resources to assure market price stability' (Davidson, 1999 [1998]: 288).

20 Observing the durability of financial crises in a wide variety of financial systems, Allen (2001) concludes that financial structure – whether intermediary-based or market-based – is a relatively unimportant factor in the development of financial crises. This sits in opposition to several authors who argue country-specific factors play a significant role in the unfolding of crisis episodes, see Corsetti and Roubini (1998a, 1998b), for example. In contrast, the two-way causality suggested by Cameron and Patrick (1967) nuances the positions in a manner that is compatible with the thesis of this study.

10 The bottom line: towards institutional indicators of financial fragility

1 Law and finance theory have increasingly moved into the arena of examining the relationship between legal systems and banking systems. The theory holds that

> historically determined differences in legal tradition influence national approaches to private property rights protection, the support of private contractual arrangements, and the enactment and enforcement of investor protection laws and…these resultant legal institutions shape the willingness of savers to invest in firms, the effectiveness of corporate governance, and the degree of financial market development.
>
> (Beck and Levine, 2003: 31; see also LaPorta *et al.*, 1998; Levine, 1998; Khan and Senhadji, 2000)

2 The theories informing the selection of tentative indicators tend to be local or partial theories of such elements as bank lending or balance of payments and address the various vulnerabilities suggested by crises occurring in the most recent two decades. See Allen *et al.* (2002: Box 1) for an overview of some of the recent academic literature; see also Davis, (1995, 1999), for example.

3 The so-called CAMELS framework identifies six groups of prudential indicators guiding the assessment of financial soundness of individual enterprises – most notably deposit-taking institutions. *C*apital adequacy, *A*sset quality, *M*anagement soundness, *E*arnings, *L*iquidity and *S*ensitivity to market risk, are indicators that acknowledge implicitly that the level of debt and hence the capital structure of the institution are critical determinants in the stability and soundness of a single financial institution (see IMF, 2000b). Accounts of the international efforts to develop macroprudential indicators include Mink and Silva (2003), IMF (2000a, 2000b, 2001), Davis (1999). The process of developing analytic and procedural tools for assessing financial system soundness is part of the joint World Bank – IMF Financial Sector Assessment Program and the related Financial System Stability Assessments.

4 The effort by the IMF is consistent with the IMF's recent efforts to establish guidelines for compiling and presenting stocks and flows for the financial corporations sector (IMF 2000a) in a manner similar to its guidelines for representing stocks and flows with the rest of the world (*Balance of Payments Manual*) and for the general government sector (*Government Finances Statistics Manual*). For a summary of measurement issues and challenges facing the creation of a coherent set of macroprudential indicators, see IMF (2000b) and Davis (1999).

5 A comprehensive set of quarterly financial accounts for the euro area is currently being developed by the European Central Bank 'primarily for the purpose of monetary policy analysis…however these data may also be used to support financial stability analysis' (Mink and Silva, 2003: 9).

6 As a means of assessing contemporaneous developments, this benefit assumes that relevant authorities, when compiling the data, are cognisant of changes as the changes are occurring and have the additional ability to assess contemporaneously the potential effects. Such requirements are considerably demanding. By way of example, consider the structural shift from narrower to broader money in the 1980s, due in part to the impact of early advances in computing technologies. Initially and for some time, the impact of this change escaped the notice of most monetary authorities attempting to control commodity inflation by targeting M1 growth. Assessments of this structural change in the demand for transactions money followed even later, see Freedman (1983), Laidler (2003a).

7 For a primer on balance sheet concepts in the context of assessing financial instability of the type experienced in recent episodes, see Allen *et al.* (2002: 12–20).

8 Demirgüç-Kunt and Levine (2001: 12) inquiring into the relative contributions of intermediated versus market-based financial systems, analyse a broad set of data from forty-eight countries for the 1980–1993 period and conclude that 'financial development matters for economic success, but financial structure per se does not seem to matter much'.

9 The importance of the financial structure on the efficacy of the transmission of central bank policies is the primary focus of the Byrne and Davis (2003) study and is a complementary line of inquiry. In general, these studies find that the higher the proportion of flexibly priced financial assets (stocks, shorter term and adjustable rate credit, for example) in the portfolios of households, the stronger the policy effect, see Borio and White (2004) for example. Studies that

disaggregate the financial structure and financial linkages have the potential to uncover the information necessary to illuminate the 'black box' of the monetary policy transmission mechanism (see Rowley and Visano, 2004). More broadly, the disaggregated balance sheet information has the potential to best illuminate the transmission of all shocks of a financial nature.

10 Systemic financial risk is that risk that

> an event will trigger a loss of economic value or confidence in, and attendant increases in uncertainty about, a substantial portion of the financial system that is serious enough to quite probably have significant adverse effects on the real economy. Systemic risk events can be sudden and unexpected, or the likelihood of their occurrence can build up through time in the absence of appropriate policy responses. The adverse real economic effects from systemic problems are generally seen as arising from disruptions to the payment system, to credit flows, and from the destruction of asset values.... In all but the most highly concentrated financial systems, systemic risk is normally associated with a contagious loss of value or confidence that spreads to parts of the financial system well beyond the original location of the precipitating shock.
>
> (Group of Ten, 2001: 126)

11 Failure to provide effective media of exchange results from the inability to manage effectively the supply of the product. This inability may derive from either the bankruptcy of primary issuers or from otherwise uncontrollable increases or decreases in supply that impact adversely on the values of the media in the exchange of either consumer products or assets. The point of this study is, however, that despite best intentions of the monetary authorities, the ability to maintain a stable value for the medium of exchange is, at times, beyond their control.

12 The historical evidence suggests that the transmission of distress works most often through the domestic banking system (see Allen *et al.*, 2002). The evolution of the financial structure promoted and supported by advances in information and communications technologies may, at some future time, reveal this, too, to be an artifact of the current financial structure. As financial systems develop, an increasing amount of financial activity is moving outside the traditional banking system and this may eventually diminish the significance of banks per se in future crises.

13 The value of loans made by deposit-taking banks to private sector debt divided by GDP 'improves upon traditional financial depth measures of banking development by isolating credit issued by banks to the private sector, as opposed to credit issued to governments or public enterprises' (Levine, 1998: 603).

14 The degree of concentration measures the extent of consolidation only insofar as consolidation takes place at the level of the firm. It omits the extent to which joint ventures and strategic alliances may create a de facto higher degree of concentration, see Group of Ten (2001).

15 Cameron (1967b) employs a similar measure as a measure of bank density, though he adopts the asset perspective. Notably, his estimates of the relative size of the banking sector suggest some support for the hypothesis that as financial systems evolve the importance of intermediated finance first rises then recedes. By his estimates (1967b: Table IX.1: 301–302), the ratio of bank assets to national income in England and Wales in 1775 was 15.2 per cent, rising to 29.6 per cent in 1825 and to 34.4 per cent in 1844. Bank assets to GDP in the United

States, by comparison, were 68.5 per cent in 1929, 58.5 per cent in 1952 and by recent estimates are now down to well below one-third.

16 Further, it is noted that most frequently, the issue is presented as part of a more conventional treatment of the tension between stability on the one hand and efficiency on the other. Bordo *et al.* (1994), as a typical example, consider the extent to which the apparent stability of the larger Canadian banks is at the expense of lower efficiency in the allocation of funds in a comparison with the American banks.

17

> [T]he *width* of a shock can be defined as the fraction of firms…or markets simultaneously affected at impact. The *depth* of a shock can be defined as the fraction of firms or markets subsequently affected by the shock during the transmission phase.
>
> (Group of Ten, 2001: 127)

18 Demirgüç-Kunt and Levine (1995), for example, estimate stock market concentration using the share of market capitalisation of the ten largest companies.

19 If banks are the only or primary financial intermediaries, total non-bank liabilities less total bank liabilities will yield a measure of those financial liabilities exchanged in financial markets. Where other financial intermediaries form a significant portion of the financial system, the above measure of total market reliance would require appropriate adjustment.

20 Of these three potential channels, Furfine (2001) and Santor (2003) identify the interbank lending market as the primary channel through which distress spreads. In its study of a sample of American large and complex banking organisations, the Group of Ten (2001: 140) conclude that through short-term interbank lending and derivatives exposures direct interdependencies 'have increased substantially' over the 1990s, that direct interdependencies 'are significantly and positively related to consolidation' through these same avenues, and that this result suggests an increase in systemic risk.

21

> For some purposes it is useful to characterize an economy in terms of its leading sectors; and a part of the technical basis for the stages of growth lies in the changing sequence of leading sectors. In essence it is the fact that sectors tend to have a rapid growth-phase, early in their life that makes possible and useful to regard economic history as a sequence of stages rather than merely as a continuum, within which nature never makes a jump.
>
> (Rostow, 1990: 14)

22 The balance sheet characterisation is limited however by the fact that it will reveal overtly only direct interdependencies arising from on-balance sheet exposures. It omits, by definition, off-balance sheet exposures and requires additional interpretation and evaluation of indirect interdependencies from correlated exposures to other sectors and markets.

23 For an example of how a series of balance sheet 'snapshots' might inform an assessment of a speculation-crisis episode, see Allen *et al.*'s (2002: Annex II) characterisation of Thailand's Intersectoral Asset and Liability Positions before and after the 1997 crisis.

24 Spotton and Rowley (1998) address this issue of methodological challenges in the context of a meta-analysis of American theories of financial crises and market volatility.

Bibliography

Alchian, A. (1950) 'Uncertainty, Evolution, and Economic Theory', *Journal of Political Economy*, 58(3): 211–221.

Allen, F. (2001) 'Financial Structure and Financial Crises', *International Review of Finance*, 2: 1–19.

Allen, F. and Gale, D. (1995) 'A Welfare Comparison of Intermediaries and Financial Markets in Germany and US', *European Economic Review*, 39: 179–209.

Allen, F. and Gale, D. (1997) 'Financial Markets, Intermediaries, and Intertemporal Smoothing', *Journal of Political Economy*, 105: 523–546.

Allen, F. and Gale, D. (2000) *Comparing Financial Systems*, Cambridge, MA: MIT Press.

Allen, M., Rosenberg, C., Keller, C., Setser, B. and Roubini, N. (2002) 'A Balance Sheet Approach to Financial Crisis', *IMF Working Paper WP/02/210*, Washington, DC: International Monetary Fund.

Andréadès, A. (1966) *History of the Bank of England 1640–1903*, 4th edn, Rep, New York: Augustus M. Kelley.

Arthur, W.B. (1988) 'Self-Reinforcing Mechanisms in Economics', in P.W. Anderson, K.J. Arrow and D. Pines (eds) *The Economy as an Evolving Complex System*, Reading, MA: Addison-Wesley.

Arthur, W.B. (1994) 'Inductive Reasoning and Bounded Rationality', *American Economics Association Papers and Proceedings*, 84(2): 406–411.

Ashton, T.S. (1948) *Industrial Revolution 1760–1830*, London, New York: Oxford University Press.

Ashton, T.S. (1959) *Economic Fluctuations in England 1700–1800*, Oxford: Clarendon Press.

Bagehot, W. (1962 [1873]) *Lombard Street: A Description of the Money Market*, Intro. F.C. Genovese, Homewood, Ill: R.D. Irwin.

Basset, W.F. and Carlson, M. (2002) 'Profits and Balance Sheet Developments at U.S. Commercial Banks in 2001', *Federal Reserve Bulletin*, June: 259–288.

Bauman, Z. (1987) *Legislators and Interpreters: On Modernity, Post-modernity, and Intellectuals*, Ithaca, NY: Cornell University Press.

Beck, T. and Levine, R. (2003) 'Legal Institutions and Financial Development', *NBER Working Paper Series No. 10126*, Cambridge, MA: National Bureau of Economic Research.

Beck, T., Demirgüç-Kunt, A. and Levine, R. (2003) 'Bank Concentration and Crises', *NBER Working Paper No. 9921*, Cambridge, MA: National Bureau of Economic Research.

Beckert, J. (1996) 'What is Sociological about Economic Sociology? Uncertainty and the Embeddedness of Economic Action', *Theory and Society*, 25: 803–840.

Bencivenga, V.R. and Smith, B.D. (1991) 'Financial Intermediation and Endogenous Growth', *Review of Economic Studies*, 58: 195–209.

Bennett, R.F. (2003) '10 Facts about Today's Economy', *Joint Economic Committee*, Online. Available HTTP: http://jec.senate.gov/economy/10FactsEconomy.pdf (accessed 24 April 2004).

Benston, G.G. (1996) 'The Origins of and Justification for the Glass–Steagall Act', in A. Saunders and I. Walter (eds) *Universal Banking*, Chicago, IL: Irwin Professional Publishing.

Berle, A. and Means, G. (1932) *The Modern Corporation and Private Property*, New York: Macmillan.

Berlin, I. (1969) *Four Essays on Liberty*, London and New York: Oxford University Press.

Bernanke, B.S. (1983) 'Nonmonetary Effects of the Financial Crisis in the Propagation of the Great Depression', *American Economic Review*, 73(3): 257–276.

Bernanke, B.S. and Gertler, M. (1989) 'Agency Costs, Net Worth, and Business Fluctuations', *American Economic Review*, 79(1): 14–31.

Bernstein, P.L. (1985) 'Does the Stock Market Overreact? Discussion', *Journal of Finance*, 40(3): 806–808.

Bernstein, P.L. (1998a) 'Stock Market Risk in a Post-Keynesian World', *Journal of Post Keynesian Economics*, 21(1): 15–24.

Bernstein, P.L. (1998b) *Against the Gods: The Remarkable Story of Risk*, New York: John Wiley.

Bibow, J., Lewis, P. and Runde, J. (2005) 'Uncertainty, Conventional Behavior, and Economic Sociology', *American Journal of Economics and Sociology*, 64(2): 507–532.

Biggart, N.W. and Beamish, T.D. (2003) 'The Economic Sociology of Conventions: Habit, Custom, Practice, and Routine in Market Order', *Annual Review of Sociology*, 29: 443–464.

Board of Governors of the Federal Reserve System (1943) *Banking and Monetary Statistics*, Washington, DC: Federal Reserve Board.

Bogen, J.I. and Krooss, H.E. (1960) *Security Credit: Its Economic Role and Regulation*, Englewood Cliffs, NJ: Prentice-Hall.

Boot, H.M. (1984) *The Commercial Crisis of 1847*, Hull: Hull University Press.

Bordo, M.D. and Wheelock, D.C. (1998) 'Price Stability and Financial Stability: The Historical Record', *Review*, St. Louis: Federal Reserve Bank of St. Louis, (September/October): 41–62.

Bordo, M.D., Rockoff, H. and Redish, A. (1994) 'The U.S. Banking System from a Northern Exposure: Stability versus Efficiency', *Journal of Economic History*, 54(2): 325–340.

Borio, C. and Lowe, P. (2002) 'Assessing the Risk of Banking Crises', *BIS Quarterly Review*, December: 43–54.

Borio, C. and White, W. (2004) 'Whither Monetary and Financial stability? The Implications of Evolving Policy Regimes', *BIS Working Paper No 147*, Basel, Switzerland: Bank for International Settlements.

Burmeister, E. (1980) *Capital Theory and Dynamics*, Cambridge: Cambridge University Press.

Byrne, J.P. and Davis, E.P. (2003) *Financial Structure: An Investigation of Sectoral Balance Sheets in the G-7*, Cambridge: Cambridge University Press.

Calomiris, C.W. and Schweikart, L. (1991) 'The Panic of 1857: Origins, Transmission, and Containment', *The Journal of Economic History*, 51(4): 807–834.

Cameron, R. (1967a) 'England 1750–1844', in R. Cameron (ed.) in collaboration with O. Crisp, H.T. Patrick and R. Tilly, *Banking in the Early Stages of Industrialization, A Study in Comparative Economic History*, New York: Oxford University Press.

Cameron, R. (1967b) 'Conclusion', in R. Cameron (ed.) in collaboration with O. Crisp, H.T. Patrick and R. Tilly, *Banking in the Early Stages of Industrialization, A Study in Comparative Economic History*, New York: Oxford University Press.

Cameron, R. (1972) *Banking and Economic Development, Some Lessons of History*, New York: Oxford University Press.

Cameron, R. and Patrick, H.T. (1967) 'Introduction', in R. Cameron (ed.) in collaboration with O. Crisp, H.T. Patrick and R. Tilly, *Banking in the Early Stages of Industrialization, A Study in Comparative Economic History*, New York: Oxford University Press.

Cardwell, D. (1995) *The Norton History of Technology*, New York: Norton.

Carosso, V.P. (1970) *Investment Banking in America: A History*, Cambridge, MA: Harvard University Press.

Carter, I. (2003) 'Positive and Negative Liberty', in E.N. Zalta (ed.), *The Stanford Encyclopedia of Philosophy*, Spring edn., Online. Available HTTP: http://plato.stanford.edu/archives/spr2003/entries/liberty-positive-negative/ (accessed 23May 2004).

Chandler, Jr., A.D. (1990) *Scale and Scope: The Dynamics of Industrial Capitalism*, Cambridge, MA: Harvard University Press.

Chant, J., Lai, A., Illing, M. and Daniel, F. (2003) 'Essays on Financial Stability', *Bank of Canada Technical Report No. 95*, Ottawa: Bank of Canada.

Clapham, J. (Sir John) (1945) *The Bank of England: A History*, Cambridge: Cambridge University Press. 2 vols.

Cohen, J.S. (1978) 'The Achievements of Economic History: The Marxist School', *Journal of Economic History*, 38(1): 29–57.

Collins, M. (1991) *Banks and Industrial Finance in Britain, 1800–1939*, Hampshire, UK: Macmillan.

Cooper, R.N. (1999) 'Comments and Discussions', *Brookings Papers on Economic Activity*, 1999(2): 280–284.

Cope, S.R. (1978) 'The Stock Exchange Revisited: A New Look at the Market for Securities in London in the Eighteenth Century', *Economica*, 45: 1–21.

Corsetti, G.P. and Roubini, N.D. (1998a) 'What Caused the Asian Currency and Financial Crises? Part I: Macroeconomic Overview', *NBER Working Paper No 6833*, Cambridge, MA: National Bureau of Economic Research.

Corsetti, G.P. and Roubini, N.D. (1998b) 'What Caused the Asian Currency and Financial Crises? Part II: The Policy Debate', *NBER Working Paper No 6834*, Cambridge, MA: National Bureau of Economic Research.

Cottrell, P.L. and Anderson, B.L. (1974) *Money and Banking in England. The Development of the Banking System 1694–1914*, Newton Abbot: David & Charles.

Davidson, P. (1982–83) 'Rational Expectations: A Fallacious Foundation for Studying Crucial Decision-Making Processes', *Journal of Post Keynesian Economics*, 5: 182–197.

Davidson, P. (1991) 'Is Probability Theory Relevant for Uncertainty? A Post Keynesian Perspective', *Journal of Economic Perspectives*, 5(1): 129–143.

Davidson, P. (1996) 'Reality and Economic Theory', *Journal of Post Keynesian Economics*, 18(4): 479–508.

Davidson, P. (1998) 'Efficiency and Fragile Speculative Financial Markets: Against the Tobin Tax and For a Creditable Market Maker', *American Journal of Economics and Sociology*, 57(4): 639–662.

Davidson, P. (1999 [1998]) 'Volatile Financial Markets and the Speculator', *Economic Issues*, reprinted in L. Davidson (ed.) (1999) *Uncertainty, International Money, Employment and Theory: The Collected Writings of Paul Davidson*, New York: St. Martin's Press, 276–295.

Davies, G. (1994) *A History of Money From Ancient Times to the Present Day*, Cardiff: University of Wales Press.

Davis, E.P. (1995) *Debt, Financial Fragility and Systemic Risk*, (Rev) Oxford: Oxford University Press.

Davis, E.P. (1999) 'Financial Data Needs for Macroprudential Surveillance – What are the Key Indicators of Risks to Domestic Financial Stability?', *Handbooks in Central Banking Lecture Series No. 2*, Bank of England: Centre for Central Banking Studies.

Davis, E.P. (2002) 'A Typology of Financial Crises', *Financial Stability Review No 2*, Austrian National Bank.

Deane, P. and Cole, W.A. (1967) *British Economic Growth, 1688–1959: Trends and Structure*, 2nd edn, London: Cambridge University Press.

De Long, J.B. (1999) 'Financial Crises in the 1890s and 1990s: Must History Repeat?', *Brookings Papers on Economic Activity*, 1999(2): 253–279.

De Long, J.B., Schleifer, A., Summers, L. and Waldmann, R.J. (1990) 'Positive Feedback Investment Strategies and Destabilizing Rational Speculation', *Journal of Finance*, 45(2): 379–395.

Demirgüç-Kunt, A. and Detragiache, E. (1998) 'The Determinants of Banking Crises in Developing and Developed Countries', *IMF Staff Papers*, 45(1): 81–109.

Demirgüç-Kunt, A. and Levine, R. (1996) 'Stock Market Development and Financial Intermediaries: Stylised Facts', *World Bank Economic Review*, 10(2): 291–321.

Demirgüç-Kunt, A. and Levine, R. (2001) *Financial Structure and Economic Growth: A Cross-Country Comparison of Banks, Markets, and Development*, Cambridge, MA: MIT Press.

Diamond, D.W. (1984) 'Financial Intermediation and Delegated Monitoring', *Review of Economic Studies*, 37: 393–414.

Diamond, D.W. and Dybvig, P.H. (1983) 'Bank Runs, Deposit Insurance, and Liquidity', *Journal of Political Economy*, 91(3): 401–419.

Dickson, P.G.M. (1967) *The Financial Revolution in England: A Study in the Development of Public Credit*, London: MacMillan.

Dimand, R.W. (2005) 'Fisher, Keynes, and the Corridor of Stability', *American Journal of Economics and Sociology*, 64(1): 185–199.

Dolar, V. and Meh, C. (2002) 'Financial Structure and Economic Growth: A Non-Technical Survey', *Bank of Canada Working Paper No. 2002–24*, Ottawa: Bank of Canada.

Dornbusch, R. (2001) 'A Primer on Emerging Market Crises', *NBER Working Paper No. 8326*, Cambridge, MA: National Bureau of Economic Research.

Dunn, S. (2000) 'Fundamental Uncertainty and the Firm in the Long Run', *Review of Political Economy*, 12(4): 419–434.

Dunn, S. (2001) 'Bounded Rationality is not Fundamental Uncertainty: A Post Keynesian View', *Journal of Post Keynesian Economics*, 23(4): 567–587.

Edgell, S. (2001) *Veblen in Perspective: His Life and Thought*, Armonk, NY: M.E. Sharpe.

Edwards, G.W. (1967 [1938]) *The Evolution of Finance Capitalism*, Rep. New York: A.M. Kelley.

Eichengreen, B. and Mitchener, K. (2003) 'The Great Depression as a Credit Boom Gone Wrong', *BIS Working Papers No 137*, Basel, Switzerland: Bank for International Settlements.

Eichengreen, B. and Portes, R. (1987) 'The Anatomy of Financial Crises Excerpt from Threats to International Financial Stability', in R. Portes and A.K. Swoboda (eds) London: Cambridge University Press.

Einzig, P. (1932) *The World Economic Crisis 1929–1931*, London: MacMillan.

Einzig, P. (1966) *Primitive Money*, 2nd edn, Oxford: Pergamon Press.

Eiteman, W.J. (1933) 'The Relation of Call Money Rates to Stock Market Speculation', *Quarterly Journal of Economics*, 47: 449–463.

Ellsberg, D. (1961) 'Risk, Ambiguity, and the Savage Axioms', *Quarterly Journal of Economics*, 75(4): 643–669.

Emmons, W.R. and Schmid, F.A. (2000) 'The Asian Crisis and the Exposure of Large U. S. Firms', *Review*, St. Louis: Federal Reserve Bank of St. Louis.

Fama, E. (1965) 'The Behavior of Stock Prices', *Journal of Business*, 38: 34–105.

Fama, E. (1991) 'Efficient Markets: II', *Journal of Finance*, 46(5): 1575–1617.

Favereau, O. (2002) 'Conventions and Regulation', in R. Boyer and Y. Saillard (eds) *Regulation Theory: The State of the Art*, London and New York: Routledge.

Fazio, R.H. (1986) 'How Do Attitudes Guide Behavior?', in R.M. Sorrentino and E.T. Higgins (eds) *Handbook of Motivation and Cognition: Foundations of Social Behaviour*, vol. 1, New York: Guilford Press.

Fels, R. (1952) 'The Theory of Business Cycles', *Quarterly Journal of Economics*, 66(1): 25–42.

Fisher, I. (1930) *The Theory of Interest*, New York: MacMillan.

Fisher, I. (1932) *Booms and Depressions*. New York: Adelphi; reprinted in I. Fisher (1997) *The Works of Irving Fisher*, vol. 10, W.J. Barber (ed.) London: Pickering & Chatto.

Fisher, I. (1933) 'The Debt-Deflation Theory of Great Depressions', *Econometrica* 1(3): 337–357; reprinted in I. Fisher (1997) *The Works of Irving Fisher*, vol. 10, W.J. Barber (ed.) London: Pickering & Chatto.

Fleisig, H.W. (1975) *Long Term Capital Flows and the Great Depression: The Role of the United States, 1927–1933*, New York: Arno Press.

Flood, R.P. and Garber, P.M. (1980) 'Market Fundamentals versus Price-Level Bubbles: The First Tests', *Journal of Political Economy*, 88(4): 745–770.

Forget, E. (1990) 'John Stuart Mill's Business Cycle', *History of Political Economy*, 22(4): 629–642.

Fortune, P. (2001) 'Margin Lending and Stock Market Volatility', *New England Economic Review*, 4: 3–25.

Freedman, C. (1983) 'Financial Innovation in Canada: Causes and Consequences', *American Economic Review*, 73(2): 101–106.

Freeman, C., Clark, J. and Soete, L (1982) *Unemployment and Technical Innovation: A Study of Long Waves and Economic Development*, Westport: Greenwood Press

Friedman, M. and Schwartz, A. (1963) *A Monetary History of the United States 1867–1960*, New York: Princeton University Press.

Froot, K.A., Scharfstein, D.S. and Stein, J.C. (1992) 'Herd on the Street: Informational Inefficiencies in a Market with Short-Term Speculation', *Journal of Finance*, 47(4): 1461–1484.

Furfine, C. (2001) 'The Interbank Market During a Crisis', *BIS Working Papers No 99*, Basl: Bank for International Settlements.

Furubotn, E.G. and Richter, R. (1991) 'The New Institutional Economics: An Assessment', in E.G. Furubotn and R. Richter (eds) *The New Institutional Economics: A Collection of Articles from the Journal of Institutional and Theoretical Economics*, Tubingen: Mohr (Siebeck).

Galbraith, J.K. (1955) *The Great Crash 1929*, London: Hamish Hamilton.

Galbraith, J.K. (1990) *A Short History of Financial Euphoria*, New York: Penguin Books.

Garber, P. (1990) 'Famous First Bubbles', *Journal of Economic Perspectives*, 4(2): 35–54.

Gayer, A.D., Rostow, W.W. and Schwartz, A.J. with the assistance of I. Frank (1975) *The Growth and Fluctuation of the British Economy, 1790–1850: An Historical, Statistical, and Theoretical Study of Britain's Economic Development*, New York: Barnes & Noble Books.

Gerschenkron, A. (1962) *Economic Backwardness in Historical Perspective*, Cambridge, MA: Belknap Press.

Ghosh, B.N. (2001) 'Financial Crisis in MIT Countries: Myths and Realities', in B.N. Ghosh (ed.) *Global Financial Crises and Reforms: Cases and Caveats*, London: Routledge.

Giddens, A. (1991) *Modernity and Self-Identity: Self and Society in the Late Modern Age*, Stanford, CA: Stanford University Press.

Gilbart, J.W. (1968 [1882]). *The History, Principles, and Practice of Banking*, New York: Greenwood Press, 2 vols.

Gilfillan, S.C. (1967 [1935]) *The Sociology of Invention*, Rep. Cambridge, MA: MIT Press.

Goldsmith, R.W. (1969) *Financial Structure and Development*, New Haven, London: Yale University Press.

Goldstein, M. (1998) 'The Asian Financial Crises: Causes, Cures, and Systemic Implications', *Policy Analyses in International Economics No. 55*, Washington, DC: Institute for International Economics.

Goodhart, C.A.E. (1972) *The Business of Banking 1891–1914*, London: Weidenfeld & Nicolson.

Graham, B. and Dodd, D. (1934) *Security Analysis*, New York: McGraw-Hill.

Graham, B., Dodd, D.L. and Cottle, S. (1962) *Security Analysis: Principles and Technique*, 4th edn, New York: McGraw-Hill.

Granovetter, M. and Swedberg, R. (1992) (eds) *The Sociology of Economic Life*, Boulder, CO: Westview Press.

Group of Ten (2001) *Report on Consolidation in the Financial Sector*, Online. Available HTTP: www.bis.org, www.imf.org and www.oecd.org (accessed 27 May 2004).

Hamouda, O. and Rowley, R. (1988) *Expectations, Equilibrium and Dynamics: A History of Recent Economic Ideas and Practices*, New York: St. Martin's Press.

Hamouda, O. and Rowley, R. (1996) *Probability in Economics*, London: Routledge.

Hawtrey, R.G. (1965 [1879]) *The Art of Central Banking*, 2nd edn, Rep. New York: Augustus M. Kelley.

Heiner, R.H. (1983) 'The Origin of Predictable Behavior', *American Economic Review*, 75(4): 560–595.

Hilferding, R. (1981 [1910]) *Finance Capital: A Study of the Latest Phase of Capitalist Development*, with an introd. by T. Bottomore (ed.), from translations by M. Watnick and S. Gordon, London: Routledge & K. Paul.

Hodgson, G. (1998) 'The Approach of Institutional Economics', *Journal of Economic Literature*, 36(1): 166–192.

Hong, H., Kubik, J.D. and Stein, J. (2004) 'Social Interaction and Stock-Market Participation', *Journal of Finance*, 59(1): 137–163.

Hoppit, J. (1986) 'Financial Crises in Eighteenth-century England', *Economic History Review*, 39(1): 39–58.

Horkheimer, M. and Adorno, T.W. (1982) *Dialectic of Enlightenment*, trans. J. Cumming, New York: Continuum.

Hughes, J.R.T. (1956) 'The Commercial Crisis of 1857', *Oxford Economic Papers*, 8(2): 194–222.

Hyndman, H.M. (1967 [1908]) *Commercial Crises of the Nineteenth Century*, 3rd edn, Rep. New York: Augustus M. Kelley.

Illing, M. and Liu, Y. (2003) 'An Index of Financial Stress for Canada', *Bank of Canada Working Paper 2003–14*, Ottawa: Bank of Canada.

IMF (2000a) *Monetary and Financial Statistics Manual*, Washington, DC: International Monetary Fund.

IMF (2000b) 'Macroprudential Indicators of Financial System Soundness', *IMF Occasional Paper No. 192*, Washington, DC: International Monetary Fund.

IMF (2001) 'Financial Soundness Indicators: Policy Paper', Washington, DC: International Monetary Fund.

IMF (2004) 'Integrating the Balance Sheet Approach into Fund Operations', Washington, DC: International Monetary Fund. Online. Available HTTP: www.imf.org/external/np/pdr/bal/2004/eng/022304.htm (accessed 07 July 2004).

Isard, W. (1942) 'A Neglected Cycle: The Transport-Building Cycle', *The Review of Economic Statistics*, November: 149–158.

Jenks, L.H. (1927) *The Migration of British Capital to 1875*, New York: Alfred A. Knopf.

Jones, C. (1993) 'The New Opposition in the House of Lords 1720–3', *Historical Journal*, 36(2): 309–329.

Kaen, F.R. and Rosenman, R.E. (1986) 'Predictable Behavior in Financial Markets: Some Evidence in Support of Heiner's Hypothesis', *American Economic Review*, 76(1): 212–220.

Kaldor, N. (1982) *The Scourge of Monetarism*, New York: Oxford University Press.

Kaufman, G.G. (1995) *The U.S. Financial System: Money, Markets, and Institutions*, 6th edn, Englewood Cliffs, NJ: Prentice-Hall.

Kelly, M. and Cormac, O.G. (2000) 'Market Contagion: Evidence from the Panics of 1854 and 1857', *American Economic Review*, 90: 1110–1124.

Keynes, J.M. (1973a [1936]) 'The General Theory of Employment, Interest and Money', reprinted in vol. VII of D. Moggeridge and E. Johnson (eds) *Collected Writings of John Maynard Keynes*, London: Macmillan.

Keynes, J.M. (1973b [1937]) 'The General Theory of Employment', *Quarterly Journal of Economics*, 51: 209–223, reprinted in E. Johnson (ed.) (1973) *The General Theory and After: Part II Defence and Development*. vol. XIV of the *Collected Writings of John Maynard Keynes*, London: Macmillan.

Khan, M.S. and Senhadji, A.S. (2000) 'Financial Development and Economic Growth: An Overview', *IMF Working Paper WP/00/209*, Washington, DC: International Monetary Fund.

Kindleberger, C.P. (1984) *A Financial History of Western Europe*, London: George Allen and Unwin.

Kindleberger, C.P. (1989) *Manias, Panics, and Crashes: A History of Financial Crises*, revised edn, New York: Basic Books.

King, M. (1999) 'Challenges for Monetary Policy: New and Old', in *New Challenges for Monetary Policy*, A Symposium sponsored by the Federal Reserve Bank of Kansas, Jackson Hole, Wyoming. Online. Available HTTP: http:// www.kc.frb.org/publicat/sympos/1999/sym99prg.htm (accessed 11 January 2000).

King, R.G. and Levine, R. (1993) 'Finance and Growth: Schumpeter Might be Right', *Quarterly Journal of Economics*, 108(3): 717–737.

Klein, B.H. (1977) *Dynamic Economics*, Cambridge, MA: Harvard University Press.

Knight, F. (1964 [1921]) *Risk, Uncertainty and Profit*, Rep. New York: Augustus M. Kelley.

Kondrateiff, N.D. (1935) 'The Long Waves in Economic Life', *The Review of Economic Statistics*, 17(6): 105–115.

Koppl, R. (1991) 'Retrospectives: Animal Spirits', *Journal of Economic Perspectives*, 5(3): 203–210.

Kuznets, S. (1930) *Secular Movements in Production and Prices*, Boston and New York: Houghton Mifflin.

Lai, A. (2002) 'Modelling Financial Stability: A Survey of the Literature', *Bank of Canada Working Paper 2002–12*, Ottawa: Bank of Canada.

Laidler, D. (1999) *Fabricating the Keynesian Revolution: Studies of the Interwar Literature on Money, the Cycle, and Unemployment*, Cambridge: Cambridge University Press.

Laidler, D. (2003a) 'The Price Level, Relative Prices, and Economic Stability: Aspects of the Interwar Debate', *BIS Working Papers No 136*, Basel, Switzerland: Bank for International Settlements.

Laidler, D. (2003b) 'Monetary Policy Without Money: Hamlet Without the Ghost', *Macroeconomics, Monetary Policy, and Financial Stability: A Festschrift in Honour of Charles Freedman*, Ottawa: Bank of Canada.

Lang, K. and Lang, G.E. (1962) 'Collective Dynamics: Process and Form', in A.M. Rose (ed.) *Human Behavior and Social Processes: An Interactionist Approach*, Boston, MA: Houghton Mifflin.

LaPorta, R., Lopez-de-Silanes, F., Schleifer, A. and Vishny, R. (1998) 'Law and Finance', *Journal of Political Economy*, 106(6): 1113–1155.

Leijonhufvud, A. (1981 [1973]) 'Effective Demand Failures', *Swedish Journal of Economics*, 75: 27–48, reprinted in A. Leijonhufvud (1981) *Information and Coordination: Essays in Macroeconomic Theory*, New York: Oxford University Press.

Leijonhufvud, A. (1998) 'Three Items for the Macroeconomic Agenda', *Kyklos*, 51: 197–218.

Levine, R. (1997) 'Financial Development and Economic Growth: Views and Agenda', *Journal of Economic Literature*, 35: 688–726.

Levine, R. (1998) 'The Legal Environment, Banks, and Long-Run Economic Growth', *Journal of Money, Credit, and Banking*, 30(3): 596–613.

Levine, R. and Zervos, S. (1998) 'Stock Markets, Banks, and Economic Growth', *American Economic Review*, 88(3): 537–558.

Lintner, J. (1965) 'The Valuation of Risk Assets and the Selection of Risky Investments in Stock Portfolios and Capital Budgets', *Review of Economics and Statistics*, 47: 13–37.

Luckett, D.G. (1982) 'On the Effectiveness of the Federal Reserve's Margin Requirement', *Journal of Finance*, 37(3): 783–795.

McCloskey, H. and Zaller, J. (1984) *The American Ethos: Public Attitudes toward Capitalism and Democracy*, Cambridge, MA: Harvard University Press.

MacLeod, H.D. (1886) *The Theory and Practice of Banking*, 4th edn, London: Longmans Green, 2 vols.

Marshall, A. (1923) *Money, Credit and Commerce*, London: MacMillan.

Marx, Karl (1971 [1859]) 'A Contribution to the Critique of Political Economy', with an introd. by M. Dobb, trans. by S.W. Ryazanskaya; M. Dobb (ed.) (1971), London: Lawrence & Wishart.

Meyersohn, R. and Katz, E. (1957) 'Notes on a Natural History of Fads', *American Journal of Sociology*, 62: 594–601.

Mill, J.S. (1965 [1848]) *Principles of Political Economy with Some of Their Applications to Social Philosophy*, in J.M. Robson (ed.) *Collected Works of John Stuart Mill*, vol II–III, 1965, Toronto: University of Toronto Press.
Mill, J.S. (1967 [1826]) 'Paper Currency and Commercial Distress', in J. Robson (ed.) vol.4, (1967) *Collected Works of John Stuart Mill*, Toronto: University of Toronto Press.
Miller, D.L. (1985) *Introduction to Collective Behavior*, Belmont, CA: Wadsworth.
Mink, R. and Silva, N. (2003) 'The Use of Financial Accounts in Assessing Financial Stability', *OECD STD/NAES/FA(2003)4*, Organisation for Economic Co-operation and Development.
Minsky, H. (1982a) *Can 'IT' Happen Again? Essays on Instability and Finance*, Armonk, NY: ME Sharpe.
Minsky, H. (1982b) 'Debt-Deflation Processes in Today's Institutional Environment', *Banca Nazionale del Lavoro Quarterly Review*, 143: 375–393.
Minsky, H. (1986) *Stabilizing an Unstable Economy*, New Haven, CT: Yale University Press.
Mints, L. (1945) *A History of Banking Theory in Great Britain and the United States*, Chicago, IL: University of Chicago Press.
Modigliani, F. and Miller, M. (1958) 'The Cost of Capital, Corporation Finance, and the Theory of Investment', *American Economic Review*, 48(3): 261–297.
Modigliani, F. and Miller, M. (1963) 'Corporate Income Taxes and Cost of Capital', *American Economic Review*, 53: 433–443.
Moore, B. (1988) *Horizontalists and Verticalists: The Macroeconomics of Credit Money*, Cambridge: Cambridge University Press.
Morgan, E.V. and Thomas, W.A. (1962) *The Stock Exchange*, London: Elek Books.
Mossin, J. (1969) 'Security Pricing and Investment Criteria in Competitive Markets', *American Economic Review*, 59: 749–756.
Neal, L. (1990) *The Rise of Financial Capitalism: International Capital Markets in the Age of Reason*, Cambridge: Cambridge University Press.
Neal, L. (1994) 'The Finance of Business during the Industrial Revolution', in R. Floud and D. McCloskey (eds) *The Economic History of Britain since 1700*, 2nd edn, Cambridge: Cambridge University Press.
Neal, L. (1998) 'The Financial Crisis of 1825 and the Restructuring of the British Financial System', *Review*, St Louis: Federal Reserve Bank of St. Louis, (May/June): 53–76.
North, D.C. (1981) *Structure and Change in Economic History*, New York: W.W. Norton.
North, D.C. (1990) *Institutions, Institutional Change, and Economic Performance*, Cambridge: Cambridge University Press.
Organisation for Economic Co-operation and Development (2004) *National Accounts for OECD Countries Vol. IIIb: Financial Balance Sheets-Stocks, 1991–2002*, Organisation for Economic Co-operation and Development.
Papadimitriou, D.B. and Wray, L.R. (2001) 'Minsky's Analysis of Financial Capitalism', in R. Bellofiori and P. Ferri (eds) *Financial Keynesianism and Market Instability*, vol. I, Cheltenham: Edward Elgar.

Perelman, M. (1999) *The Natural Instability of Markets: Expectations, Increasing Returns, and the Collapse of Capitalism*, New York: St. Martin's Press.

Phongpaichit, P. and Baker, C. (2000) *Thailand's Crisis*, Chiang Mai: Silkworm Books.

Pigeon, M-A. (2004) 'Interest Rate Setting at the Bank of Canada: Setting the Agenda', in M. Lavoie and M. Seccareccia, (eds) *Central Banking in the Modern World: Alternative Perspectives*, Cheltenham: Edward Elgar.

Pollock, D. (1998) 'Introduction: Making History Go', in D. Pollock (ed.) *Exceptional Spaces: Essays in Performance and History*, Chapel Hill: University of North Carolina Press.

Pressnel, L.S. (1956) *Country Banking in the Industrial Revolution*, Oxford: Clarendon Press.

Rabin, M. (1998) 'Psychology and Economics', *Journal of Economic Literature*, 36 (1): 11–46.

Radelet, S. and Sachs, J.D. (1998) 'The East Asian Financial Crisis: Diagnosis, Remedies, and Prospects', *Brookings Papers on Economic Activity*, 1998(1): 1–90.

Richards, R.D. (1929) *The Early History of Banking in England*, London: Westminster.

Robertson, D.H. (1928) 'Theories of Banking Policy', *Economica*, 8: 131–146.

Robertson, D.H. (1949 [1926]) *Banking Policy and the Price Level: An Essay in the Theory of the Trade Cycle*, Rep. New York: Augustus M. Kelley.

Rosenberg, N. (1976) *Perspectives on Technology*, Cambridge: Cambridge University Press.

Rosenberg, N. (1994) *Exploring the Black Box: Technology, Economics, and History*, Cambridge: Cambridge University Press.

Rosenberg, N. and Birdzell, Jr., L.E. (1986) *How the West Grew Rich*, New York: Basic Books.

Roseveare, H. (1991) *The Financial Revolution, 1660–1760*, London: Longman.

Rosovsky, H. (1965) 'The Take-Off into Sustained Controversy', *Journal of Economic History*, 25(2): 271–275.

Rostow, W.W. (1975) 'Kondratieff, Schumpeter, and Kuznets: Trend Periods Revisited', *Journal of Economic History*, 35(4): 719–753.

Rostow, W.W. (1990) *The Stages of Economic Growth: A Non-communist Manifesto*, 3rd edn, Cambridge: Cambridge University Press.

Rowley, R. and Visano, B.S. (2004) 'Monetary Dialogue and Dogma in the Bank of Canada: Inside Evidence Revisited', in M. Lavoie and M. Seccareccia (eds) *Central Banking in the Modern World: Alternative Perspectives*, Cheltenham: Edward Elgar.

Sahel, B. and Vesala, J. (2001) 'Financial Stability Analysis Using Aggregate Data', *BIS Papers No. 1*, Basel Switzerland: Bank for International Settlements.

Samuels, W.J. (1995) 'The Present State of Institutional Economics', *Cambridge Journal of Economics*, 19: 569–590.

Samuelson, L. (2004) 'Modeling Knowledge in Economic Analysis', *Journal of Economic Literature*, 42(2): 367–403.

Santor, E. (2003) 'Banking Crises and Contagion: Empirical Evidence', *Bank of Canada Working Paper 2003–1*, Ottawa: Bank of Canada.

Santos, J.A.C. (2000) 'Bank Capital Regulation in Contemporary Banking Theory: A Review of the Literature', *BIS Working Papers No. 90*. Basel, Switzerland: Bank for International Settlements.

Scharfstein, D.S. and Stein, J.C. (1990) 'Herd Behavior and Investment', *American Economic Review*, 80(3): 465–479.

Schliefer, A. and Vishny, R.W. (1986) 'Large Shareholders and Corporate Control', *Journal of Political Economy*, 96(3): 461–488.

Schubert, E.S. (1988) 'Innovations, Debts, and Bubbles: International Integration of Financial Markets in Western Europe, 1688–1720', *Journal of Economic History*, 48(2): 299–306.

Schumpeter, J.A. (1939) *Business Cycles: A Theoretical, Historical, and Statistical Analysis of the Capitalist Process*, New York: McGraw-Hill, 2 vols.

Schumpeter, J.A. (1994 [1954]) *History of Economic Analysis*, edited from manuscript by E.B. Schumpeter; introduction by M. Perlman, New York: Oxford University Press.

Schwartz, A. (1988) 'Financial Stability and the Federal Safety Net', in W. Haraf and R.M. Kushneider (eds) *Restructuring Banking and Financial Services in America*, Washington: American Enterprise Institute.

Shackle, G.L.S. (1949) 'A Non-Additive Measure of Uncertainty', *Review of Economic Studies*, 17: 70–74.

Shackle, G.L.S. (1955) *Uncertainty in Economics*, Cambridge: Cambridge University Press.

Shackle, G.L.S. (1970) *Expectation Enterprise and Profit*, London: George Allen & Unwin.

Sharpe, W.F. (1964) 'Capital Asset Prices: A Theory of Market Equilibrium under Conditions of Risk', *Journal of Finance*, 19(3): 425–442.

Shiller, R. (2002) *Irrational Exuberance*, Princeton, NJ: Princeton University Press.

Simmel, G. (1957) 'Fashion', *American Journal of Sociology*, 62(6): 541–558.

Simmel, G. (1990 [1907]) *The Philosophy of Money*, 2nd edn, trans. T. Bottomore and D. Frisby, D. Frisby (ed.) London: Routledge.

Simon, H. (1959) 'Theories of Decision-Making in Economics', *American Economic Review*, 49: 253–283.

Simon, H. (1978) 'Rationality as Process and Product of Thought', *American Economic Review*, 68: 1–16.

Smelser, N.J. (1963) *Theory of Collective Behavior*, New York: Free Press.

Snyder, C. (1930) 'Brokers' Loans and the Pyramiding of Credit', *Journal of the American Statistical Association*, 25(169a): 88–92.

Soros, G. (1987) *The Alchemy of Finance*, New York: Simon and Schuster.

Sorrentino, R.M. and Roney, C.J.R. (2000) *The Uncertain Mind: Individual Differences in Facing the Unknown*, London: Psychology Press.

Spotton, B. (1997) 'Financial Instability Reconsidered: Orthodox Theories versus Historical Facts', *Journal of Economic Issues*, 3(1). 175–195.

Spotton, B. and Rowley, R. (1996) 'Monetary Dialogue and Dogma in Canada: The Inside View', *Canadian Business Economics*, 5(1): 20–32.

Spotton, B. and Rowley, R. (1998) 'Efficient Markets, Fundamentals, and Crashes: American Theories of Financial Crises and Market Volatility', *American Journal of Economics and Sociology*, 57(4): 663–690.

Stiglitz, J.E. (1969) 'A Re-Examination of the Modigliani–Miller Theorem', *American Economic Review*, 59(5): 784–793.

Stiglitz, J.E. (1972) 'Some Aspects of the Pure Theory of Corporate Finance: Bankruptcies and Take-Overs', *Bell Journal of Economics*, 3(2): 458–482.

Stiglitz, J.E. (1973) 'Taxation, Corporate Financial Policy and the Cost of Capital', *Journal of Public Economics*, 2: 1–34.

Stiglitz, J.E. (1974) 'On the Irrelevance of Corporate Financial Policy', *American Economic Review*, 64(6): 851–866.

Stiglitz, J.E. and Weiss, A. (1981) 'Credit Rationing in Markets with Imperfect Information', *American Economic Review*, 71(3): 393–410.

Swedberg, R. and Granovetter, M. (1992) 'Introduction', in M. Granovetter and R. Swedberg (eds) *The Sociology of Economic Life*, Boulder, CO: Westview Press.

Temin, Peter (1976) *Did Monetary Forces Cause the Great Depression?*, New York: W.W. Norton & Company.

Thomas, W. (1935) 'Use of Credit in Security Speculation', *American Economic Review*, 25: 21–30.

Thompson, E.P. (1963) *The Making of the English Working Class*, New York: Vintage Books.

Thompson, E.P. (1985 [1977]) *Whigs and hunters: The Origin of the Black Act*, Rep. Harmondsworth: Penguin Books.

Tooke, T. (1838) *History of Prices, and the State of Circulation, from 1793 to 1837*. Rep. New York: Adelphi Company.

Townsend, R.M. (1990) *Financial Structure and Economic Organization: Key Elements and Patterns in Theory and History*, Cambridge, MA: Basil Blackwell.

Turner, R.H. and Killian, L.M. (1987) *Collective Behavior*, 3rd edn, Englewood Cliffs, NJ: Prentice Hall.

Van Wincoop, E. and Yi, K-M. (2000) 'Asia Crisis Postmortem: Where Did the Money Go and Did the United States Benefit?', *FRBNY Economic Policy Review*, September: 51–71.

Veblen, T. (1904) *The Theory of Business Enterprise*, New York: Charles Scribner's Sons.

Veblen, T. (1912) *The Theory of the Leisure Class: An Economic Study of Institutions*, New York: MacMillan.

Viner, J. (1936) 'Recent Legislation and the Banking System', *American Economic Review*, 26: 106–119.

Visano, B.S. (2002) 'Toward a Socio-Economic Perspective on Financial Manias and Panics', *American Journal of Economics and Sociology*, 61(4): 801–822.

Visano, B.S. (2003) 'Electronic Payments and Exchange Rate Regimes: Industry Changes and the Question of a Single North American Currency', in L.P. Rochon and M. Seccareccia (eds) *Dollarization: Lessons from Europe for the Americas*, London and New York: Routledge.

Visano, B.S. (2004) 'Financial Crises, Crashes, and Speculative Bubbles: The Regulation Imperative in a Critique of Recent Episodes', in P. O'Hara (ed.) *Global Political Economy and the Wealth of Nations: Performance Institutions, Problems and Policies*, London and New York: Routledge.

Von Peter, G. (2004) 'Asset Prices and Banking Distress: A Macroeconomic Approach', *BIS Working Papers No 167*, Basel, Switzerland: Bank for International Settlements.

Ward-Perkins, C.N. (1950) 'The Commercial Crisis of 1847', *Oxford Economic Papers*, 2(1): 75–94.

Weber, M. (1947) *The Theory of Social and Economic Organization*, trans. A.M. Henderson and T. Parsons, New York: Free Press.

Weber, M. (1992 [1904]) *Protestant Ethic and the Spirit of Capitalism*, trans. T. Parsons; introduction by A. Giddens, London and New York: Routledge.

White, E. (1983) *The Regulation and Reform of the American Banking System, 1900–1929*, Princeton, NJ: Princeton University Press.

White, E. (1986) 'Before the Glass-Steagall Act: An Analysis of the Investment Activities of National Banks', *Explorations in Economic History*, 23: 33–55.

Wicksell, K. (1936 [1898]) *Interest and Prices: A Study of the Causes Regulating the Value of Money*, trans. R.F. Kahn, London: MacMillan.

Wicksell, K. (1978 [1935]) *Lectures on Political Economy*, vol. II, Rep. Fairfield: Augustus M. Kelley.

Williams, J.B. (1965 [1938]) *The Theory of Investment Value*, Rep. New York: Augustus M. Kelley.

Wood, Douglas (1983) 'Review', *The Economic Journal*, 93(371): 685–686.

Index